FINANCIAL MIRACLES
and the
NEW FINANCIAL NATURE

Douglas C. Knisely, CPA

WESTBOW
PRESS®
A DIVISION OF THOMAS NELSON
& ZONDERVAN

WestBow Press books may be ordered through booksellers or by contacting:

WestBow Press
A Division of Thomas Nelson & Zondervan
1663 Liberty Drive
Bloomington, IN 47403
www.westbowpress.com
844-714-3454

Scripture marked (NKJV) taken from the New King James Version®. Copyright © 1982 by Thomas Nelson. Used by permission. All rights reserved.

Scripture quotations marked (NIV) are taken from the Holy Bible, New International Version®, NIV®. Copyright © 1973, 1978, 1984, 2011 by Biblica, Inc.® Used by permission of Zondervan. All rights reserved worldwide. www.zondervan.com The "NIV" and "New International Version" are trademarks registered in the United States Patent and Trademark Office by Biblica, Inc.®

ISBN: 978-1-9736-9909-5 (sc)
ISBN: 978-1-9736-9908-8 (hc)
ISBN: 978-1-9736-9907-1 (e)

Library of Congress Control Number: 2023909649

Print information available on the last page.

WestBow Press rev. date: 06/01/2023

Miracles are a retelling in small letters of the very same story which is written across the whole world in letters too large for some of us to see.
—C. S. Lewis
"God in the Dock"

～

Faith does not, in the realist, spring from the miracle but the miracle from the faith.
—Fyodor Dostoevsky
"The Brothers Karamazov"

～

Knowing there's one thing I still haven't told you: I now believe, by the way, that miracles can happen.
—Nicholas Sparks
"A Walk to Remember"

～

Miracles, in the sense of phenomena we cannot explain, surround us on every hand: life itself is the miracle of miracles.
—George Bernard Shaw
"The Collected Plays of George Bernard Shaw"

CONTENTS

INTRODUCTION

I have set the LORD always before me;
Because He is at my right hand I shall not be moved.
—Psalm 16:8 (NKJV)

This verse is part of the Old Testament of the Bible, written by David. David was a man after God's own heart, according to another Bible passage. Can you imagine being a man after God's own heart?

We know the heart of God is love because one passage says that God is love. We also know the heart of God is justice. Passages tell of the judgment separating the sheep from the goats based on the good or evil we do. God is also mercy, as told by the story of the Good Samaritan, who helped an injured man while religious leaders passed by on the other side of the road. Religion means nothing if it does not serve to change the heart.

God loves to save the lost, as illustrated by the shepherd who left the ninety-nine sheep in the pasture in order to find and save the one lost sheep. We read that there is joy in heaven when the lost are found and repent. One passage says that God desires to save everyone.

It would be exciting to be a man or woman after God's own heart, with a nature of love, justice, mercy, and compassion for the lost. But although David's life was lived with a heart after God's own heart, there were many areas of his life that were filled with struggle, tumult, and sin.

David struggled to escape the sword of Saul, the anointed king. Saul hunted David in the wilderness. On one occasion, God provided a miracle that kept Saul and his soldiers asleep while David took Saul's spear. David used it to confront Saul the next day, demonstrating how David had spared Saul's life. God withdrew support for Saul because of Saul's disobedience, replacing him with David. God may withdraw support for us and our nation because of disobedience.

David was involved in adultery with Bathsheba, a married woman. When she became with child, David sent her husband to the front line of a battle, to be killed by the enemy. After David's sincere repentance, God forgave him and the relationship was restored. Nevertheless there was punishment: the baby died, and David's family life became one of dysfunction and tragedy.

The goal of this book is help you not to be moved or shaken when financial loss, suffering, and bad news come your way. David's psalm will be our guide as we strive to become men and women after God's own heart. Soon we will understand that salvation, which means to be saved from sin, is accomplished by God's grace through faith. Faith is a gift from God.

We understand that David's life of struggle, tumult, and sin mirrors our lives. Our lives will be restored through repentance when we attempt to turn in a righteous direction and seek forgiveness.

As a man or woman after God's own heart, you will not be moved, because the Lord is always at your right hand to provide and guide. Imagine driving to work and being hit from behind, totaling your car but leaving you uninjured. The Lord is at your right hand, keeping you calm and helping you handle the situation with upright thinking. You are sharing information with the other party, taking note of the positions of the cars, writing down license plate numbers, and calling the police. You calm the other party. You stop the swearing. You show restraint. God is with you during this misfortune and will be with you as you recover. You will not be moved or shaken because you will have complete confidence that God, in the form of His Son, Jesus, and the Holy Spirit, will be at work in your circumstances.

God is at your right hand, providing comfort and direction, because you always set the Lord before you. Setting the Lord before you is a major emphasis of this book. Doing so causes you to understand financial and relationship miracles. Putting the Lord always before you is the task of coming to Jesus Christ, to receive his blessings and power.

The power of the Holy Spirit coming upon you changes your entire nature, including what you think. With the Holy Spirit, you become a new person—not with an amended nature, but a new nature. Your entire life is turned upside down. The things and activities that used to consume your time will no longer satisfy. Spending changes as priorities change. Time commitments change, conversations change, parenting techniques change, and a "New Financial Nature" is formed.

You will not be shaken or moved, because God is at your right hand. An angel stands beside its subject. This happens because you always set God before you.

This book is a journey to an understanding of God in our financial lives as we become born-again, receiving the "New Financial Nature".

Douglas C. Knisely, CPA

CHAPTER ONE

GOD IS POWERFUL AND PROVIDES

A RAGING FINANCIAL STORM

The raging sea and wind, the surging waves against the dock, the churning seashore, and the threatening billows combine to form a visual image of the financial turmoil we may be trying to endure at this time. We are looking for a ray of hope, a ray of sunshine to pierce the dark clouds. We seek financial relief or perhaps a turnaround in business or employment. We want anything to grasp and hold tight to that declares God still loves us and will provide for us, even in the midst of the storm. We believe that God is powerful and can calm the storm.

JESUS CALMS THE STORM

A perfect representation of this is the event described in Luke 8 of Jesus in a boat crossing a lake (see vv. 22–25). As the disciples sailed, Jesus fell asleep. The boats used in biblical times were about seven feet wide, thirty feet long, and four feet deep. They were powered by both oars and sail.

My father had a similar-sized boat that he used on Lake Erie for fishing and entertainment. It was difficult for me to stand and fish when the boat was moving at low speed or even idling, because of the constant, gentle waves. So it is hard for me to imagine sleeping in Dad's boat, even though it had cushions in the bow. Being tired enough to fall asleep in such a boat is an example of the humanity of Jesus. He was that exhausted.

While Jesus slept, a windstorm came down on the lake, causing massive waves to fill the boat with water. But Jesus continued to sleep until the disciples woke Him with shouts that they were perishing. Jesus rebuked the wind and waves, and the sea became calm. This is an example of the divinity of Jesus.

Jesus then said to the disciples, "Where is your faith?" He scolded them, criticizing their attitude and mindset. It was like a dad disciplining his son: "Why did you do that? What were you thinking? We don't behave that way. We are a family; we work together, trust each other, and provide help to each other."

I always try to follow these disciplines. One instance I remember was when I was in college and renting an apartment with my good friend, whom I had known for years. It was the last quarter for me. I would be moving out and leaving the apartment and my furniture for him. He would continue to live there, alone, until the lease ran out. Of course, there was a question of my share of the rent that would accrue after my departure. One day he said, "I was thinking you wouldn't pay the rent."

I exclaimed, "Oh, Smithy! Don't you know me by now? I fully intend to pay everything to the end of the lease, even though I will not be living here!"

Jesus experienced the same dismay with the disciples who doubted him. "Boys! Don't you know me by now? Don't you know I love you and care for you? Have you seen me show compassion and love to a widow and raise her son from the dead? (see Lk 7:11–16.) Have you seen me heal diseases and cast out unclean spirits? (see Lk 6:17–19.) Will I not show the same willingness and compassion for you?"

Our God is a powerful God, who can calm any financial storm. Jesus loves us; He helps us with our schedules, work load, services, and energy. Calming the sea was a miracle that saved lives. More importantly, it was a sign for us to believe that Jesus is the Son of God. It demonstrated the power of God available for the lives of those who believe. Jesus rebuked the wind and the raging waters. And Jesus is still with us because He said so.

There are two fears in this passage. One is fear of the storm— the surge, the wind, the rocking boat, and the fear of drowning. This can be associated with the financial fears we have today— loss of a job, conflicts with colleagues, differences with the boss, and fear of losing the ability to pay our bills, resulting in debt, humiliation, and bankruptcy.

The second great fear occurs after the calming of the storm, when Jesus sits down. The disciples turn to one another in fear and trembling, saying, "Who is this who can speak to the wind and waves, and they listen and obey?"

When the crisis and financial fear is resolved, we should have the same response: who is this who can create a business sale at the end of the day? Who can suddenly provide us workers on short notice? Who can put a bag of groceries at our front door?

The financial miracle that reverses the crisis and gives light at the end of the tunnel requires recognition and praise. We must relax at the end of the day and think of all the meetings, conversations, and exchanges that went well, without a problem. And we should thank God for all the little things.

Most little things that happen throughout the day are miracles disguised as everyday happenings. When you think about it, each breath we take is a miracle going into the lungs, putting good air into the bloodstream and exhausting bad air. How can we explain the exchanges brought about by each breath?

Our God is powerful. He is willing to help us, is in the boat with us, and is beside us in our troubles. Trust Jesus. Get to know Jesus and His promises. Remember the little things He does each day. Lean on Him for solutions. Pray, knowing that fear of the Lord is the fountain of life (see Prv 14:27).

Come into the kingdom of heaven and find salvation. When Jesus first started His mission, He said for us to repent because the kingdom of heaven is at hand (see Mt 4:17). There is a different way of life in the kingdom of heaven, where sins are forgiven by Jesus Christ, and we are saved.

This is best described when the apostle Paul was freed from prison by a mighty act of God. The jailer was aware that God was among them and asked Paul about the things we need to do to be saved. Paul probably took the jailer by surprise when he said that there were no great tasks. God only requires us to believe in the Lord Jesus Christ (see Acts 16:30–31). There is only one step: believe that the Lord Jesus Christ is who He says He is. He is the Son of God, who died for your sins and rose again from the dead.

John MacArthur provides a clear visual. The kingdom of heaven refers to the sphere of salvation. Jesus urges listeners to seek salvation—and with it will come the full care and provision of God (cf. Rom 8:32; Phil 4:19; 1 Pt 5:7).[1]

POINT OF VIEW

There is life in the world, the normal life of activity: buying, selling, working, saving, giving, and caring. The activities of life in the world have the point of view of the world, the expectations of the world, and the satisfactions of the world. We expect a return for our efforts. In work, that return is cash. In volunteerism, it is recognition. In the home, it is respect. In spending, it is good value for a fair price.

That sounds like a peaceful life, except when the expectations are not fulfilled. On the other hand, a man who is not regenerated is never satisfied. We are born selfish and greedy. We seek power and authority. These normal human desires are caused by sin, which is rebellion against God and the commandments He put in place as a standard for living. The first commandment is to love and fear God with all your heart, soul, energy, and mind. The second is to love your neighbor as yourself.

In contrast, the promise of life in Christ has a different point of view, a different perspective, and a different aura. All activities are God-breathed, God-activated, and godly in thought, word, and deed. Life has a new purpose, which is for the glory of God. Life has a new meaning, which includes forgiving, thinking of eternal life, and becoming a new creation through the Holy Spirit. In addition, there is a new security, a new sense of God being in control around us, a feeling of safety in the midst of a storm, a new calmness, a new hope, a new friendship with the living God, and a new confidence that prayers are reaching God through our mediator, Jesus Christ. This personal new creation is a life raft in the financial storm, which I call the "New Financial Nature". "Therefore, if anyone *is* in Christ, *he is* a new creation; old things have passed away; behold, all things have become new" (2Cor 5:17 NKJV).

I demonstrated this new point of view when I was in the emergency room several years ago. I was in an examining room, separated from other rooms by curtains. When I am in an exam room, I try to be a good patient and not complain about the waiting, the lack of privacy, or the fancy gowns that are required so the nurses and doctors can access my body. Eventually a nurse, a registration lady, and a doctor came in. The doctor called for a CAT computer axial tomography (CAT) scan and oxygen tube.

So I began to get dressed in one of the fancy gowns. When I took off my pants, I put them on a post attached to the wall. An oxygen technician came in, put the tube in my nose, and turned on the oxygen. Later an orderly arrived to take me on the bed to the CAT scan room. I had my eyes closed, and I was resting while he set up. The oxygen technician came in again to adjust the oxygen, and away I went.

When I came back, I saw my pants were still dangling from

the post. The back pocket was hanging at about eye level. I checked my wallet and saw that I had been robbed of seventy dollars. What was my reaction? What would your reaction be? Would you cry out, "I've been robbed? Call the police!" There are always security people around in an emergency room, it seems. Would you insist an investigation be started?

My reaction was different. I pitied the thief and thought, "We live in a sinful world." I did nothing but lie back down in the bed. I did not disrupt the emergency room full of sick patients.

Most people would have been angry. However, when an individual is regenerated "in Christ," priorities change. We accept the fact that bad things happen to good people. Through faith we know God can provide through thick and thin, including robbery. With each loss or struggle, say to yourself, "I wonder how God will handle this situation?"

JESUS PROVIDES FISH

The story of Jesus providing a catch of fish is taken from Luke 5:5–11. A multitude was pressing around Jesus to hear the Word of God. Jesus saw two boats standing by and the fishermen cleaning their nets. He got into one of the boats and asked to be put out from shore, to teach the multitudes. When He stopped speaking, He turned to Simon, one of the fishermen, and told him to head out into deeper water and let down the nets for a catch.

Simon complained, saying he had fished all night and caught nothing.

It is easy to complain. Complaining is our natural inclination because we are selfish. Our own agenda takes first priority.

I was in a small accounting practice as a partner. I recall the receptionist and typist telling me that it was inconvenient to come to work. This was years ago, when there were no computers, just typewriters. Generally people were thankful to have jobs.

Simon complained but reconsidered when he thought of who

was asking. This reaction is similar to our behavior when the big boss asks—we general put aside our own agenda and do as we are told. Simon had watched Jesus heal and teach in the synagogue. He had gained respect for Jesus. Simon responded to Jesus by calling him Master. Simon said, "Because you say so, I will let them down."

After returning the nets to the boat and going out into deeper water, Simon and the other fishermen let down the nets. They caught such a large number of fish that the nets were beginning to break. They called for help from others. The number of fish taken in filled both boats.

Simon and his partners were filled with joy and awe. They realized their fishing skills had very little to do with the miraculous catch. Astonished, and beginning to notice that they were in the presence of God, they fell on their knees, saying, "Away from me, Lord, because I am a sinful man."

A financial miracle in our lives should evoke the same response: astonishment, unworthiness, thankfulness, and worship.

It is hard for general employees to relate to the significant effect of a miracle of sales. The point of view of the sole owner of a business is different because the small business owner has planned, organized, purchased inventory, built a store, received business loans, and used all personal savings, putting everything on the line in hope of sales and a financial return. When a miracle of sales is received, the heart pounds, the smile turns on, and the owner and family are elated. Then there is worship, because the miraculous sales were beyond the owner's capabilities and only possible with God's intervention.

My father and his partner built a truck stop, where they sold diesel fuel and truck products like oil and tires. We lived in a house behind the station and could watch some of the activity. He was just starting the business when one morning we looked out the window and saw sixteen trucks had parked in the parking lot overnight. We were elated that Dad had some business.

Another aspect of this passage is that God requires participation in a financial miracle. The disciples had to use their fishing skills and the tools available, including the nets and the boat. God does not throw the fish into the boat. People pray for financial miracles, expecting cash to be suddenly deposited into the bank account or a great-aunt to die and leave an inheritance. God does not work this way, in my experience. God guides, directs, provides ideas, and lights fires, but He does not make it easy. God provides the body, the mind, and the human skills. Many skills require development. All must be used to serve others.

Serving others is an important lesson. In a book about financial security and success the author made the statement, "Find a need and fill it."[2] Think of all the things and services an individual or family needs during the day. Develop a product or service to fill a gap that would make life easier.

One passage of scripture says to seek first God's kingdom and His righteousness, and all other things will be added to you (see Mt 6:33). In God's kingdom, people serve and love each other as we want to be served and loved. Focus on serving others, and you will receive. Even in a large company, each employee has a task to serve others in the department. Please do the best you can do.

The catch of fish is a financial miracle for a small business owner—an owner who has struggled all night without success, an owner who is exhausted, an owner who is ready to give up for the day.

The fishermen were challenged by someone on the beach to put the net on the right side of the boat in order to find fish. Can you imagine the response of the fishermen? "Who are you to tell us how to fish? Where do we put the net? Can't the fish get to the net on the left side of the boat? And we are tired!"

These are the questions we all have for the person who has a new idea. We struggle and toil, worrying about cash flow, juggling who and who not to pay first, and racking our brains as to how to increase sales. We have always worked this way. The new way will cost us. God requires participation in a financial miracle. Sometimes just following up on a mistake will make the difference.

I remember a friend coming up to me, somewhat excited. She manufactured a disk that was cut from a sheet of material, probably a dozen at a time. She sold them to a customer who used the disks in his own manufacturing process. Each disk was consumed during this process.

At the end of the week, my friend had some leftover material, enough for a partial batch. But the material had to be processed sideways instead of straight. She sent the disks over to the customer. He called her to say the sideways disks were not consumed as rapidly, saving the customer a great deal of time and money. She was excited about this development and told me the story. The new process would give her product more value to the customer and a competitive edge in the marketplace.

What is the difference between putting the net on the other side of the boat and putting the material in sideways? The result is the same: a financial miracle. This is the way God works, in my experience. God sets you up in a situation just to see what you will do, how you will react. He tests you to see if you will utilize new information.

I prayed to God for another illustration to expand the story of the fishermen, and a day later I remembered the woman and the disks. Praise God.

The bases of the financial miracle of the catch of fish are obedience, listening, and trying again, even if we are tired, hungry, and irritable. How many financial miracles have we pushed away because we did not try one more time in a different way?

To understand the power of God available in our lives and to participate in a financial miracle, it seems to me we first must get close to God and hear what He says. Then, in obedience and fear, we must make the effort to put the boat out into deeper waters and let out the net on the other side of the boat, as instructed.

ATTRIBUTES OF GOD

The disciples in fear of the raging storm cried to Jesus for help, just as we, in our raging financial storm, cry to God for help. Our cries for help are caused by our personal helplessness and failure to combat and defend ourselves against the circumstances we face. We look to a greater power, someone outsides ourselves, for deliverance. We look for someone we can trust, to whom we can speak about our problems. We seek someone who will listen, love us, and actually help. It is helpful to review the power and attributes of God, to whom you will pray for a financial miracle. Our God is powerful and innovative, with a love for us and a desire to help us. God wants us to depend on Him; He wants to help.

God is the creator and sustainer of the universe. God created the universe out of nothing. God sustains the world: the sun keeps shining, the earth keeps spinning, and the crops keep growing. God reveals Himself through the physical universe, showing order, consistency, uniformity, complexity, and understandability. We respond in awe. "For since the creation of the world His invisible *attributes* are clearly seen, being understood by the things that are made, *even* His eternal power and Godhead, so that they are without excuse" (Rom 1:20 NKJV).

Defining the term "God," R. A. Finlayson says that in His Being, God is self-existing. While His creation is dependent on Him, He is independent of His creation. He not only has life, but He is the source of life to His universe. He has the source of that life within Himself. Finlayson gives an example of the burning bush where Moses met God (see Ex 3:2). The bush was on fire but was not being consumed, showing Moses that the fire was independent of the bush. The source of the energy to fuel the flame was self-fed. God is self-existing.[3] "Have you not known? Have you not heard? The everlasting God, the LORD, The Creator of the ends of the earth, Neither faints nor is weary. His understanding is unsearchable. He gives power to the weak, And to *those who have* no might He increases strength" (Is 40:28–29 NKJV).

Since the existence of God cannot be proven using scientific methods, God's existence is taken by faith. Knowledge of God comes to us by God's self-revelation through physical nature and, more importantly, through God's revealed Word, the Bible. Through the inspired written Word, God reveals Himself, culminating in the revelation of God through Jesus Christ.

> Jesus said to him, "Have I been with you so long, and yet you have not known Me, Philip? He who has seen Me has seen the Father; so how can you say, 'Show us the Father'? Do you not believe that I am in the Father, and the Father in Me? The words that I speak to you I do not speak on My own authority; but the Father who dwells in Me does the works." (Jn 14:9–10 NKJV)

The human mind cannot understand God because God is infinite. Humans are finite, with limitations in understanding, reasoning, and logic. Nevertheless, we can know God by his activities and attributes as revealed in the Bible. *Nelson's Illustrated Bible Dictionary* provides information on the attributes of God.[4] His attributes can be grouped into two groups, according to Finlayson: natural attributes and moral attributes.

NATURAL ATTRIBUTES OF GOD

God is spirit without body or measurable form, invisible, but became visible in His Son, Jesus Christ (see Jn 4:24).

God is changeless. Although progress and activities change, He Himself is changeless (see Heb 1:12). Otherwise He would not be perfect. Therefore what we know of God, we know with certainty; He is not different from one time to another.

God is all-powerful. He creates and sustains all things and can do anything that is not inconsistent with His nature, character, and purpose. Any limitation is self-imposed (see Gn 18:14, 26). God is all-knowing and possesses all knowledge simultaneously. God knows the thoughts and motives of every heart (see Job 37:16; Ps 147:5; 1 Chr 28:9). God is everywhere. He is not confined to one part of the universe but is present at every point and moment (see Ps 139:7–12). God does not belong to one nation or generation. He is the God of all the earth (see Gn 18:25). God is eternal. Eternity refers to God's relation to time. Past, present, and future are known equally to Him (see 2 Pt 3:8; Rev 1:8). Time is like a parade that man sees only a segment at a time. God sees time in its entirety.

MORAL ATTRIBUTES OF GOD

God is holy. He is separated and exalted above other things (see Is 6:1–3). "Holiness" refers to moral excellence, which God demands of His children and which He supplies. Holiness is a gift that we receive by faith through His Son, Jesus Christ (see Eph 4:24).

God is righteous, which refers to His affirmation of what is right as opposed to what is wrong. The Ten Commandments are His moral laws, giving guidance to human conduct. God also judges the world in righteousness, meaning He brings punishment to the wicked and disobedient (see Rom 2:6–16; Dt 32:4). God's righteousness is also redemptive; God declares the believer to be in a state of righteousness because of the sacrificial death of Jesus on our behalf.

God is love, which is the essential and self-giving nature of God. God's love for man seeks to awaken a responsive love of man for God. God loved and suffered by giving His all on the cross for the redemption of humanity, desiring good for all His creatures (see Gn 1:31; Ps 145:9; Mk 10:18).

God is truth. All truth, whether natural, physical, or religious, is grounded in God. Any seemingly inconsistent teaching between physical sciences and God's revelation of Himself is more apparent than real.

God is wisdom, which means doing the best thing in the best way at the best time for the best purpose (see 1 Tim 1:17). God's divine wisdom is revealed in history, creation, redemption, human lives, and Christ.

A discussion of the attributes of God brings us hope. We realize that God loves us and can help us in many ways. He chooses, knowing what is best for us, even though we cannot understand why God would let us suffer. Our true hope is the hope of everlasting life and glorification in the welcoming arms of Jesus Christ, a hope that is above all the suffering and discord of earthly existence. In a study of near-death experiences, during which an individual dies and comes back to life through resuscitation, one of the common experiences is the overwhelming experience of unconditional love, to the point where the individual does not want to return to life on earth.

God is powerful to help us. With this knowledge, we cry out for financial help. However, many of us are separated from God. God refuses to hear us because of our sin. Sin creates a barrier separating us from God. "Then one said to Him, 'Lord, are there few who are saved?' And He said to them, 'Strive to enter through the narrow gate, for many, I say to you, will seek to enter and will not be able'" (Lk 13:23–24 NKJV).

CHAPTER TWO

GOD REQUIRES PARTICIPATION

MIRACLES WITH PARTICIPATION

In our quest for financial miracles, we dream of the final result, visualizing a large home, a happy family, college scholarships for the children, a car that always starts, a corner office, and other wealth outcomes. We overlook and avoid the thought that financial miracles require participation. Jesus required human participation and signs of faith before performing a miracle.

Practicing Christians have believed in miracles since the foundation of Christianity. The central Christian miracle is the death and resurrection of Jesus Christ, true God and true man, who sacrificed His life and died for our sins, satisfying the wrath of God. God hates sin. He requires only the perfect individual to be received into heaven, which perfection and the robe of righteousness come to us through faith in Jesus Christ. Therefore, inherent in the faith of the practicing Christian is the creation of the world, the virgin birth, the miracles or signs of Christ, the resurrection, the sending of the Holy Spirit, and the Holy Spirit speaking to the writers of the Bible, among other miracles. There is no room for skepticism for the practicing Christian. The greatest reason for believing in miracles is the omnipotence of almighty God. J. D. Spiceland mentions that biblical miracles have a clear objective: they are intended to bring the glory and love of God into bold relief. He continues saying they are intended, among other things, to draw man's attention away from the mundane events of everyday life and direct it toward the mighty acts of God. The Gospels teach that the miracles of Jesus Christ are prophesied works of the Messiah, and are signs of wonder to those who have the spiritual discernment to recognize them as such.[1]

The miracles in the Bible run contrary to the *observed* processes of nature, according to Augustine. They teach that our knowledge of nature is limited. Miraculous events are not correctly conceived of as irrational disruptions of the pattern of nature, but only as disruptions of the *known* part of nature.[2]

THE MAN BORN BLIND

The miracle of the man born blind is described in the gospel of John. The question about the miracle is this: are disabilities caused by sin, whether on the part of the disabled person or that person's parents? Are financial disabilities caused by sin?

As Jesus was passing by, He saw a man who had been blind from birth. His disciples asked Him if this man had sinned or his parents had sinned that he was born blind. The answer Jesus give was that neither had sinned, but that the man was available for the work of God (see Jn 9:1–3).

Jesus refuted the idea that sin was a direct cause of the blindness. Many parents feel guilt when a deformity occurs in their child, making themselves personally liable for the circumstance: "We should have done this or we should have stopped that and the child would have been normal." Then, through the difficulty of caring for the child, the works of God are revealed.

Remember the story of Helen Keller, who was born unable to

see or hear? The exasperation of her parents was overwhelming. They brought in a private teacher, Anne Sullivan, when Keller was six years old. Keller became an author and educator and cofounded the American Civil Liberties Union to improve treatment of the deaf and blind.

Perhaps your disability can likewise be overcome with innovation to be used for the glory of God. God loves you and desires for you to experience wholeness in heaven, which is our ultimate hope.

Continuing with the story of the man born blind, Jesus spat on the ground and made clay, which He put on the man's eyes. Jesus told him to wash in a nearby pool. The man came back seeing (see Jn 9:6–7).

The man born blind had to participate in the healing miracle. This is often the case in the miracles of Jesus, who used earthly resources and provided instructions. The man allowed Jesus to touch him, allowed his face to be smeared with mud mixed with saliva, and listened to instructions. The man was obedient and washed in the Pool of Siloam. The result was a healing miracle.

I am suggesting that if you desire a financial miracle, then you must participate. You must prepare yourself for the miracle, follow instructions, follow advice, seek wisdom, arouse your energy, excite your passions for the task, confront your fears, work to increase your skills, exert yourself, motivate yourself, and push yourself into the arena to do battle for your miracle.

Religious leaders questioned the man born blind because the day he was healed was the Sabbath. According to the religious leaders, Jews should not work on the Sabbath. Since healing was considered work, the opening of the eyes of a blind man on a Sabbath could not have been an act of God. The man who could now see refuted the Pharisees, saying that we know that God does not hear sinners, but if anyone is a worshipper of God and does His will, God hears him. If Jesus were not from God, He could do nothing (see Jn 9:29–33).

The important point for our discussion is verse 31, "Now we know that God does not hear sinners; but if anyone is a worshiper of God and does His will, He hears him" (Jn 9:31 NKJV). If we are praying for a financial miracle, perhaps we should understand that God does not listen to sinners. He listens to the godly person who does His will. In other words, our prayers may be redirected from reaching their target (God) by sin in our lives. We need to confront our sin and seek forgiveness before our prayer for a financial miracle will reach God through Jesus Christ, our mediator. This concept of a prayer not reaching God is consistent with other Bible passages.

> If I regard iniquity in my heart, The Lord will not hear. (Ps 66:18 NKJV)

> The LORD *is* far from the wicked, But He hears the prayer of the righteous. (Prv 15:29 NKJV)

> But your iniquities have separated you from your God; And your sins have hidden *His* face from you, So that He will not hear. (Is 59:2 NKJV)

Remember the first words of Jesus as He began His ministry? The words of Jesus were that we should repent, because the kingdom of heaven is at hand. Jesus came to earth and was crucified on the cross, accepting the wrath of God and punishment for the sins of the world. How many in your family understand what sin is? How many understand that Jesus suffered and died for their sins in order to set them free from being a slave to sin?

Jesus sets us free to be people of God and to receive His mercy and hope. We bring this mercy and hope into our lives through repentance. After repentance, we ask God for forgiveness. The Holy Spirit then begins the indwelling process.

In my church, we receive forgiveness of sins each week. We

kneel as a congregation and recite the words of confession, saying, "I have sinned in thought, word, and deed and deserve temporal and eternal punishment, but I am sorry for them and plead for mercy and forgiveness."

The pastor responds, "By my office as a called and ordained minister of the church, I declare unto to you the entire forgiveness of all your sins in the name of the Father, Son, and Holy Spirit. Amen." The mighty act the church offers each week is the forgiveness of sins. It is possible to downplay the sermon, the liturgy, the music, and the fellowship, and yet seek each week the forgiveness of sins. Find a church with a theology that forgives sin.

SIN

Asking for repentance indicates that there is something for everyone to repent of. Perhaps we should review some ideas about sin. I wrote a book titled *Financial Sin and the "New Financial Nature"*, expanding on the many everyday ways we financially sin.

Do you fear God? Do you love God, think about God each day, depend on Him each day, consider Him your closest friend, work for His glory, and seek His righteousness? If not, you sin.

Does your language reflect righteousness? Do you always speak kind and courteous words, lifting up the individual and providing encouragement? Do you speak positively, in a normal tone of voice? If not, you sin.

Do you eagerly look forward to Sunday worship, enjoy singing hymns or godly songs, listen closely to the scripture lesson, pay attention to the sermon, participate in baptism and Holy Communion, and enjoy reading the Bible and religious books? If not, you sin.

Do you honor your father, mother, teachers, policemen, and others in authority by obeying their direct instructions, considering them your leaders, and giving thanks for their public service? If not, you sin.

Do you kill your neighbors, if not with weapons, then with words of criticism or harassment? Do you use foul language, bullying tactics, angry reactions, and dishonorable deeds? If you act this way, you sin.

Do you commit adultery, if not the actual act, then by lusting after a married person, thinking of sexual fantasies, participating in dishonorable relations, or failing to keep the marriage bed pure? If you act this way, you sin.

Do you steal others' property, use legal tricks to redirect ownership rights, use political power to disband a business, pass laws to eliminate competition, take small items from work, use time at work for personal telephone calls, take long lunch breaks, oppress the poor, fail to pay wages on time, or do damage to your neighbors' property? If you act this way, you sin,

Do you lie about your neighbor, gossip at work, make up stories to save yourself, twist actual results, tamper with records, tamper with the results of scientific research, give false testimony, lie to the public, lie to your spouse, or commit deceit? If you act this way, you sin.

Do you desire your neighbor's property? Are you unhappy with the things you have? Do you desire the workers of a competitor? If you act this way, you sin.

Who can escape from the actions above? No one. We are all sinners. But God has a plan.

GEORGE MÜLLER

Mr. George Müller was a Christian evangelist who set out to prove that God hears and answers prayer. God put it in his heart to establish an orphanage. With prayer alone, he established and sustained the orphanage, keeping a diary of its needs and how God supplied those needs. He never asked anyone for money but called upon God alone to provide.

This information is from Wikipedia. The New Orphan Houses,

commonly known as the Müller Homes, were an orphanage in the district of Ashley Down, north of Bristol, England. They were built between 1849 and 1870 by the Prussian evangelist George Müller to show the world that God not only heard but answered prayer. The five houses held up to 2,050 children at a time. Some seventeen thousand children passed through their doors before the buildings were sold to Bristol City Council in 1958. Müller never made requests for financial support, nor did he go into debt, even though the five homes cost over a hundred thousand pounds to build. By the time he died in 1898, Müller had received 1.5 million pounds through prayer and had had more than ten thousand children in his care.

As an example of financial miracles, here is a story is taken from Mr. Müller's diary. Notice that his prayers requested specific actions and were for the benefit of others, not self-seeking.

It was towards the end of November 1857, when I was most unexpectedly informed that the boiler of our heating apparatus at No. 1 leaked very considerably, so that it was impossible to go through the winter with such a leak. Our heating apparatus consists of a large cylinder boiler, inside of which the fire is kept, and with which boiler the water pipes, that warm the rooms, are connected. Hot air is also connected with this apparatus. The boiler had been considered suited for the work of the winter. To suspect that it was worn out, and not to do anything towards replacing it by a new one, and to have said, I will trust in God regarding it, would be careless presumption, but not faith in God. It would be the counterfeit of faith.

The boiler is entirely surrounded by brickwork; its state, therefore, could not be known without taking down the brickwork;

this, if needless, would be rather injurious to the boiler, than otherwise; and as for eight winters we had had no difficulty in this way, we had not anticipated it now. But suddenly, and most unexpectedly, at the commencement of the winter, this difficulty occurred. What then was to be done? For the children, especially the younger infants, I felt deeply concerned, that they may not suffer, through want of warmth. But how were we to obtain warmth? The introduction of a *new* boiler would, in all probably, take many weeks. The *repairing* of the boiler was a questionable matter, on account of the greatness of the leak; but if not, nothing could be said of it, until the brick-chamber in which it is enclosed, was, at least in part, removed; but that would, at least, as far as we could judge, take days; and what was to be done in the meantime, to find warm rooms for 300 children?

It naturally occurred to me, to introduce temporary gas-stoves; but on further weighing the matter, it was found, that we should be unable to heat our very large rooms with gas, except we had many stoves, which we could not introduce, as we had not a sufficient quantity of gas to spare from our lighting apparatus. Moreover, for each of these stoves we needed a small chimney, to carry off the impure air. This mode of heating, therefore, through applicable to a hall, a staircase, or a shop, would not suit our purpose. I also thought of temporary introduction of Arnott's stoves; but they would have been unsuitable, requiring long chimneys (as they would have been of a temporary kind) to go out the windows. On this account, the uncertainty of their answering in our case, and the disfigurement of the rooms, led me to give up this plan also. But what was to be done? Gladly I would have paid 100 pounds, if thereby the difficulty could be overcome, and the children not be exposed to suffer for many days from being in cold rooms. At last I determined on falling entirely into the hands of God, who is very merciful and of tender compassion, and I decided on having the brick-chamber opened, to see the extent of the damage, and whether the boiler might be repaired, so as to carry us through the winter.

The day was fixed when the workman were to come, and all the necessary arrangements were made. The fire, of course, had to be let out while the repairs were going on. But now see. After the day was fixed for the repairs a bleak North wind set in. It began to blow either on Thursday or Friday before the Wednesday afternoon, when the fire was to be let out. Now came the first really cold weather, which we had in the beginning of that winter, during the first days in December. What was to be done?

The repairs could not be put off. I now asked the Lord for two things, that He would be pleased to change the North wind into a South wind, and that he would give to the workmen 'a mind to work'; for I remembered how much Nehemiah accomplished in 52 days, while building the walls of Jerusalem, because 'the people had a mind to work'. Well the memorable day came. The evening before the bleak North wind still blew: but on the Wednesday, the south wind blew: exactly as I had prayed. The weather was so mild that no fire was needed. The brickwork is removed, the leak is found out very soon, the boiler makers begin to repair in good earnest.

About half-past eight in the evening, when I was going home, I was informed at the lodge, that the acting principal of the firm, whence the boiler makers came, had arrived to see how the work was going on, and whether in any way he could speed the matter. I went immediately, therefore, into the cellar, to see him with the men, to seek to expedite the business. In speaking to the principal of this, he said in their hearing, 'the men will work late this evening, and come very early again tomorrow'.

'We would rather, Sir,' said the leader, 'work all night.' Then remembered I the second part of my prayer, that God would give the men 'a mind to work.' Thus it was: by the morning the repair was accomplished, the leak was stopped, though with great difficulty, and within 30 hours the brickwork up again, and the fire in the boiler; and all the time the south wind blew so mildly, that there was not the least need of a fire.

Here, then, is one of our difficulties which was overcome by prayer and faith.[3]

Allow me to say a few words about this miracle, which came about by prayer and faith. To suspect the boiler was worn out and not do anything about it, Müller says, would not be faith but counterfeit faith. Each day we have problems of all kinds with repairs, things not working correctly, improper manufacturing, faulty wiring, improper installation, and improper use. We are not to sit back and say, "It is God's problem, and I have faith He will fix it." God requires participation. George Müller worked hard to search for alternatives, researched different heating systems, and talked to professionals, all for the benefit of the children. He did not want them to suffer because of the cold.

We likewise should research, inquire, talk to specialists, plan, organize, and think through to overcome our obstacles. Continue praying through all your activities, asking for tools to do the work, for ideas to solve the complexity, for cooperation among suppliers, and for the right people to come together at the right time, with the right equipment, at the right cost, to do the right thing.

Notice that only after extensive decision-making and effort did George Müller put the burden on God to support his decision. He asked God for two necessary elements: that the wind would come from the south to bring warm weather, and that the workmen would have the desire to work.

It is easy to visualize a financial miracle coming to a person based solely on that person's desire to work. The desire to work is an anomaly in today's world. Someone mentioned to me that his unemployment benefits (based on the wages he earned in a previous union construction job) were higher than the wage he could earn in a nonunion replacement job. He intended to stay on unemployment for the maximum allowable period, which was thirty-nine weeks at the time. This attitude does not represent a desire to work. It demonstrates a desire to take advantage of the money in government coffers and lax laws about unemployment. His attitude is also against the teaching of the Bible, which requires each person to work for a living. In a way, his attitude is one of scamming, cheating, and slothfulness. Everyone wants something for nothing. Furthermore, this man worked for cash while receiving unemployment compensation, which is cheating the government out of benefit money and income taxes. It is stealing.

Someone came up to me recently and asked if I wanted to see a financial miracle. I said, "Of course!" She showed me a letter from a major hospital network. The letter read that after a review of her situation, the hospital was reducing her obligation to zero. She was excited and gave praise to God. She was not afraid to ask for relief. Hospitals usually are required to benefit the community if they are and wish to remain not-for-profit organizations. For patients without insurance, medical bills are often extremely large because they do not have the benefit of an insurance company negotiating reduced fees. So the poor are hit with higher bills.

Incidentally, do not pay a medical bill with a credit card, because the hospital does not charge interest. A hospital will often negotiate with you, accepting a small monthly payment. In addition, many hospitals offer forgiveness of debts.

Managing debt is one of the most common financial problems we all face. The improper use of credit cards is an easy trap that catches us off guard. It is so very easy to buy on credit, and it seems so harmless at the time. But when the bill comes, we go into shock. We don't remember the purchases or the satisfaction those purchases gave us.

One idea is always to pay off the entire card balance at the end of the month to avoid late charges, usurious interest rates, and the humiliation associated with financial trouble and worry. To prepare for the bill, in the middle of the month determine the outstanding balance and write a check for that amount. Set the check aside in an envelope. This will eliminate some worry. The check will keep your household spending up to date, and you will be more confident about money matters. Remember to deduct the check amount from your checking balance, of course. When the bill finally comes, you will have already paid a portion, reducing your anxiety.

If you have many cards with high balances, you might consider working with a consumer credit counseling company (CCCC). Such a company has made prearrangements with the credit card companies to lower interest rates and payments. The idea is to make one payment to the CCCC. They disburse the amount to the individual credit card companies at a reduced interest rate.

I worked for a consumer credit counseling company at one time. I prepared a cash income list for the customer and then prepared a detailed list of their credit card balances and minimum payments, as well as other monthly payments. We determined the net cash flow or deficit and then used the database of credit card companies and their agreements to lower interest rates and payments. The system helped many people. I also provided information on budgeting, reducing insurance premiums, and the availability of government programs to reduce heating costs.

Receiving the "New Financial Nature" has the effect of eliminating high consumer debt by changing the heart. The heart is changed to the point that much of one's old spending is not needed because greater satisfaction is available without the things we buy. We become content without extra purchases; we use what we have and are content in our situation.

CHAPTER THREE

POVERTY, GOOD NEWS, AND WORK

POOR

We are each poor, and we are each rich. It depends on definitions, statistics, and accounting for property ownership and entitlements. One definition Funk & Wagnalls gives for *poor* is that it is the term used to designate those for whom it is a struggle to procure the necessities of life.

The *Encyclopedia Britannica* offers further explanation:

> Poverty is said to exist when people lack the means to satisfy their basic needs. In this context, the identification of poor people first requires a determination of what constitutes basic needs. These may be defined as narrowly as "those necessary for survival" or as broadly as "those reflecting the prevailing standard of living in the community." The first criterion would cover only those people near the borderline of starvation or death from exposure; the second would extend to people whose nutrition, housing, and clothing,

though adequate to preserve life, do not measure up to those of the population as a whole. The problem of definition is further compounded by the noneconomic connotations that the word poverty has acquired. Poverty has been associated, for example, with poor health, low levels of education or skills, an inability or an unwillingness to work, high rates of disruptive or disorderly behavior, and improvidence.[1]

In an article printed in 2018, *USA Today* listed Liberia as the poorest country in the world, with a gross national income (GNI) per capita of $710. The second-poorest country in that year was the Central African Republic, with a GNI per capita of $730.[2]

Considering the above information, ask yourself: Are you rich or poor? In your mindset, consider yourself rich by comparing your income with the income of people in Liberia. There will always be people and families worse off than we are. Our response should be thankfulness for the things, family, and situation we have. We should not focus on things we do not have. In many countries, clean water is hard to find and requires miles of walking. In all circumstances, we are called to be thankful instead of feeling lowly, insignificant, uncared for, and sorry for ourselves. We should think of ourselves as rich—rich enough to help others, rich enough to set an example for others to follow. We should use each day to be productive and achieving.

The apostle Paul has a marvelous statement in the book of Philippians. He says that he has learned to be content in all circumstances with experience of both plenty and want. He says he has found the secret for being content in any situation. Can you imagine being content in his situation, considering all the trials he endured?

What was Paul's secret? He says he draws his strength from God. God always meets our needs. Our hearts learn to eliminate nonessentials and use the resources we have. In Paul's case, he was thankful to the churches that provided him money and food just when he needed them. God will provide for you also.

Speaking of nonessentials, I am older now and in estate-planning mode. I think about how to transfer titles to property; how to bequeath goods easily, without attorney fees; how to treat family equally; and how to get rid of stuff.

At one time, years ago, when people married, they picked out designs for fine china and tableware. Each family attending the wedding could buy one place setting and together complete the entire set. After my parents died, I inherited their fine china set. Since we have enough china, we tried to sell the set. It was expensive, made in Germany, purchased in the 1960s I think, and included serving platters and the like. No one offered to buy this beautiful set, even when I offered it online. Finally I gave it to an auction shop, which sold the entire set for sixty-five dollars, if I recall correctly. None of the family members wanted the set, including children, cousins, and in-laws.

The point is that what we hold dear due to fond memories—the cup from the museum, the collectible porcelain figurines, the silver platter, the signed football—are often of no value to a future generation. In fact young people take pride in leaving a smaller footprint in the world. It is difficult to get rid of stuff. Thank God for charitable organizations that recycle, reuse, and provide for those without.

Let us return to the definition of *poor*. If we use the definition that includes lack of education as a criterion, then are we poor? If you suddenly realize your family has access to free education, then your response should be not only thankfulness, but recognition of free education as a financial miracle. It seems to me we can encourage our children to be thankful for America's role in providing free education. If lack of education is what places you in the poor category, then diligently attend to your education, putting forth real effort.

Consider the case of Ben Carson, the surgeon who miraculously separated conjoined twins. He also ran for president of the United States, and later became the director of the United States Department of Health and Human Services. Ben Carson was from a poor household, and he was a poor student until his mother motivated him and his brother to broaden their reading. Gradually, education became interesting and fun.

GOOD NEWS

The Bible writes of good news to the poor.

John the Baptizer was put in prison because he rebuked King Herod for marrying Herod's brother's wife. John the Baptizer announced the coming of the Messiah and made the way straight. He baptized people for the forgiveness of sins in the River Jordan.

John sent two of his disciples to find out if Jesus was the Messiah. The disciples came back, having been directed by Jesus to tell of the things they saw and heard. Please note the order of the witness: the blind see, the lame walk, the lepers are cleansed, the deaf hear, the dead are raised, and the poor have the gospel preached to them (see Mt 11:2–5).

J. W. McGarvey says that Jesus sums up his work in the form of a climax, wherein preaching the gospel to the poor stands superior even to the raising of the dead. He adds that attention to the poor has always been a distinctive feature of Christianity. Therefore, to care for the poor is above miracles.[3]

Jesus, Son of God, lived a humble life on earth. He associated with the poor, had dinner with outcasts, taught the poor, selected disciples from among the poor, and was born in a stable among animals. Jesus loves the poor and was poor.

Here is an example of the poorness of Jesus. Jesus was not obligated to pay the temple tax, but he paid it anyway so as not to offend the Pharisees. How many of us pay a tax so as not to offend the tax collector and cause him embarrassment? The problem was that Jesus had no money on him. To fund the tax, Jesus told a disciple to go fishing. The disciple was to cast a hook into the sea and take the first fish that he caught. In the mouth of the fish, he would find a piece of money that would be enough to pay the temple tax for both the disciple and Jesus (see Mt 17:27).

Notice that it took work to get the money, even though the money was a gift from God. Peter had to use his fishing skills and catch the fish. God will provide you a financial miracle, but you will have to participate. It will take work.

Say it to yourself: "Jesus loves me." Jesus, Son of God, has all power, has all knowledge, and has presence everywhere at the same time. This God loves you. This is incredible, fantastic, marvelous, and wonderful; it is good news to the poor! It is a miracle.

See the wealth around you or on the other side of town. The wealthy say that God has blessed them because everyone can see their fancy cars, large homes, tended yards, suits and dresses, and other fancy possessions. Does God love the wealthy more than He loves the poor?

God is not partial. There are scripture references describing His total impartiality. Nevertheless, the angels grandly proclaimed the birth of Jesus to the shepherds in the fields, watching their flocks overnight. An angel of the Lord brought good news of great joy to all peoples (see Lk 2:8–11).

The message of great joy for all was first announced to the poor, but it is for everyone. Don't you understand that this message makes all the difference in the world?

We are freed from the chains of wealth and poverty. We are liberated to become joyful and thankful. We can praise God in our humility. Wealth and poverty have nothing to do with blessings from God. God loves us regardless of our financial circumstances. This is a financial miracle.

We are accepted and received into heaven based on our faith, not on our worldly works, political privilege, contributions, employment titles, educational degrees, summer houses, or technological gadgets. Salvation means that God has provided a way to remove our sins, be restored to fellowship, be united with people in Christ, and receive righteousness earned by Jesus Christ's sacrifice on the cross. Heaven is our hope and our desire. In heaven there are no tears and no pains. Our way to heaven is through faith in Jesus Christ, which faith is a gift.

We are saved by grace, which means salvation is not earned; it is free. It is brought about by God's love and has nothing to do with wealth or poverty. Faith is a gift from God (see Eph 2:8–10).

God desires for us to depend on Him. Remember the manna in the wilderness, which was delivered each day and twice as much on the day before the Sabbath so that the Israelites could observe the day of rest (see Ex 16:15). The Israelites were forced to depend on God for daily bread. God was teaching us that we can depend on Him. God provides.

So who is more likely to depend on God, the poor or the rich? All fervent prayer begins with helplessness and need. Who is more likely to be in a position of offering fervent prayer, the poor or the rich? God wants us to be persistent in prayer. Remember the corrupt judge and the persistent widow who finally received justice (see Lk 18:1–8)? So who is more likely to cry out in persistent prayer, the poor or the rich? Pride is a hindrance to seeking God (see Hos 7:10) and often originates in possession of power (see Lev 26:19). So who is more likely to be filled with pride, the poor or the rich?

God desires and seeks our prayer and supplication. It is amazing that God wants to hear from us and is concerned about us. He wants us to be anxious for nothing. He wants to provide for everything by prayer and supplication. With thanksgiving, let our requests be made known to God (see Phil 4:6).

I gave a speech once during Holy Week breakfast gatherings. I was talking about how God provides. As an illustration, I counted how many meals God had provided over my life. Assume I was forty at the time and that I had eaten three meals a day for three hundred and sixty-five days a year for those forty years: 3 x 365 x 40 = 43,800. I pointed out that these meals were provided during times of war, unemployment, underemployment, college, marriage, fatherhood, transfer, recession, civil unrest, national emergency, and other conditions. My emphasis was on trusting God and working with Him through prayer and supplications. The number of meals provided was a confirmation and proof that God does provide.

Months later, I was riding with someone who had attended that speech. The lady told me how much my emphasis on God providing had meant to her and her husband. Her husband had just lost his job, and the whole family was anxious about provision. Make the calculation yourself and think of all the situations in your life in which God provided. Will God stop providing? The sun comes up each day, and the earth keeps spinning.

Whenever you are depressed or without hope, put your faith in God. The sun will come out tomorrow. Just wait one more day.

I spoke with a lady who homeschools her children because of the secular and liberal emphasis in public schools. She mentioned that six suicides had occurred in the public schools, which were located in a wealthy neighborhood. Her husband taught in the public schools and discovered that a student was suicidal. He wrote a note to the student that included the words "God loves you." The phrase "God loves you" was discovered by the school administration, and he was reprimanded with the threat of dismissal.

God is powerful. He can change hearts to stand up against bullying. He can dismiss the forced regimen of liberal ideas and inclusiveness pushed onto students. Teach your children the Ten Commandments and the power of the gospel message in order to fight against Satan in the schools.

Be sure your children are solidly grounded in the knowledge that God loves them and is able to provide for them in any situation. Dismiss those who bully as mindless creatures doing inappropriate and ugly things. They do not deserve a response. Do not let your children, the next generation, become devoid of divine support.

RESPONSIBILITY

Who is responsible for providing support for the poor? There are many passages in the Bible calling for care and support for widows, orphans (the fatherless), and the poor. However, who is responsible for this support, and are there priorities in responsibilities?

Scripture says that God shows no partiality, takes no bribes, and administers justice for the fatherless and the widow. God also loves the stranger, giving him food and clothing (see Dt 10:17–18).

God sustains, defends, watches over, pleads, and seeks. He is not partial, accepts no bribes, loves the foreigner, and testifies against those who do not fear Him. God loves you and has your back. But how does God work? How are these wonderful actions implemented?

The Bible has a hierarchy of responsibilities for taking care of the poor. Let me list three priorities:

1. Individuals must meet their own needs, and the excess beyond meeting their own needs is to be given to others.
2. The others who come second are one's own family, extending down to children, across to siblings, and across to a spouse's family,
3. The third priority is the church as a community of believers caring for one another in love.

In the passages and discussion below, not once is the government listed as a responsible party involved in providing for the needs of the poor. America, with its vast welfare system redistributing the earnings of the productive to the less fortunate, is not biblical. Government is not listed in the Bible as a responsible party. The apostle Paul addressed a problem in the church with his second letter to the Thessalonians (see 2 Th 3:6–10). The problem was that people were idle, which stemmed from the doctrine of the second coming of Christ. The second coming is the decisive action of God in final judgment and salvation. The people expected this final judgment and salvation to occur promptly. Therefore the question came up: "Why should I strive, work, and suffer if my salvation is at hand? When I am in heaven, all things will be made new."

The answer is that no one knows when the second coming will happen. Therefore you ought to follow Paul's example. He was not disorderly, nor did he eat anyone's bread free of charge. Paul worked night and day, that he might not be a burden.

Therefore, in accordance with scripture, each of us should strive not to be burden on society, but to be a good example of citizenship, hard work, and industriousness (see 2 Th 3:6–15). There is no place for idleness and slothfulness in the church or among the people of God. In full confirmation of this command, Paul said that if anyone will not work, neither shall he eat.

Paul was informed that there were some among them who were living in a disorderly manner and were busybodies (see 2 Th 3:6). My motto is to be productive and to achieve each day. Effort and work in our particular callings are required. We are to be good stewards of the land and to work for the glory of God in all that we do.

Another notion of idleness comes to mind in which all personal needs are supplied by others, to the extent that one does not need to work to be satisfied. This happens in a charitable culture or a country with vast supporting programs for the needy, to the point that an individual can deliberately decide to be part of the group of needy as a personal choice of lifestyle. In a discussion I had with a leader of a large social service agency that provided homeless shelters, food pantries, low-income housing, and other benefits, he said that as benefits increase, the homelessness of an individual becomes institutionalized. The person continues permanently in the lifestyle, having no motivation to change and accepting that this is a normal way of life. They become comfortable living with others in the same situation.

This seems to be the state in America. We occasionally hear of stories of welfare recipients passing down a welfare way of life for generations. The government wants welfare recipients to increase in order to provide more jobs for the people who hand out benefits. Welfare workers vote for greater government involvement.

Ralph Drollinger has pertinent comments concerning the establishment of priorities. He says that this passage (see 2 Th 3:6-15) provides us with a foundational starting point, revealing whom God has assigned to be the primary caretaker to provide basic necessities for living. He points out that in verse 10, the apostle Paul writes that even when he was with them, he commanded them that if anyone refused to work, that same person should not eat. This is a strong statement and a command, not an option. Work is not a suggestion, says Drollinger; we are to be personally disciplined in order to meet our own needs![4]

The subject of discipline probably includes disorder, deliberate idleness, interference with the work of others, asking for handouts, and expecting others to give them necessities because they were brothers in Christ. Paul's response to this behavior was to withdraw from the disorderly and unproductive. He separated the workers who were fulfilling their responsibilities from the idle, the acknowledged believers from the busybodies.

It seems to me that welfare payments are a trap or a drug—an inviting cigarette that seems fun, relaxing, and harmless, and is in fact helpful for calming the nerves. In reality, welfare payments change the attitude, move one to dependence on government, put oneself under the authority of a caseworker, and start a downward spiral away from productive activity. The welfare lifestyle encourages involvement with gangs, boils one in self-pity, and ruins one's future.

During my time with the consumer credit counseling agency, I counseled one lady who received four hundred dollars a month from the government as a rent subsidy. If she started a job, she would lose the subsidy. I ran the numbers, assuming she had a minimum-wage job, and deducted all the normal federal, state, and city taxes, including social security, to prove she would be much better off financially by working. I told her that working is a great opportunity to become independent and self-sufficient, with the chance for promotions after establishing behavior as a good worker. The lady refused to leave the government subsidy. She was afraid of moving away from a consistent and trustworthy welfare benefit.

A point of fact is that the government cannot be trusted. Laws can change at a moment's notice. Put your trust in God with a firm foundation. God has given you many talents and energy for serving others. God is able to help you specifically when you pray with specific requests that are consistent with His purpose for your life.

In my thinking, this lady refused to work because of low self-confidence, low self-esteem, lack of encouragement, fear of entering the workforce, and belief in negative comments about her and people in her situation. I believe this is the result of the welfare system and caseworkers. Caseworkers need cases to work in order to keep their jobs. Therefore there is an incentive among government employees to keep people from succeeding and moving into the workforce.

In the Beginning, Man Had Work

"The LORD God took the man and put him in the Garden of Eden to work it and take care of it" (Gn 2:15 NIV). God desires for us to work. Work is not punishment; work is part of being in the image of God.

Adrian Rogers discusses the Christian view of daily work. Rodgers says that all daily work can be sacred. The Bible says in Proverbs 14:23 that there will be a profit when we work hard. Our work should be a blessing, not a source of boredom; dignity, not drudgery; meaningful, not monotonous.

Rodgers says that we've artificially divided work up into the secular and the sacred, but the Bible doesn't do that. Our job ought to be our place of ministry, our place of service to the Lord Jesus. Where we work is to be our temple of devotion and our lampstand for witness.

Paul wrote to the Ephesians about work, "Slaves, obey your earthly masters with respect and fear, and with sincerity of heart, just as you would obey Christ" (Eph 6:5 NIV). According to Rodgers every Christian should regard his or her work as sacred. We need to realize that when we go to the job, we're working not only for our employer, but also for Jesus.[5]

When we go to work, we are representing our families in our communities, our neighborhoods, and our alma maters. We demonstrate our values and our belief.

The financial miracle that moves people out of poverty is to discover work or create work by starting a new business. Discover an unmet need and fill it. Remember, all work is sacred and beneficial. For the Christian, work represents a witness in the community. God desires for us to be productive, with a firm understanding of the power of God, who desires for us to depend on Him. God fed the nation of Israel in the wilderness, demonstrating that He cares and has the power to provide. God provides through human effort; the Israelites had to gather and cook the manna. In addition, God put restrictions on the work of gathering, since gathering was not allowed on the Sabbath, the day of rest.

God is able to provide. If we draw near to God, He will draw near to us (see Jas 4:8). God does not operate like a magician whom you call upon in an emergency, expecting immediate deliverance.

You would not ask the president of General Motors for a favor and expect immediate results. You would not expect any results at all, not even a reply. Why? Because the president of General Motors does not know you. First we must establish a relationship, develop trust, understand each other, and communicate with each other. We must talk, listen, and wait.

Many people, I surmise, figure that God owes them a financial miracle because they are God's children. They were baptized, they belong to a church, they have never killed anyone, and they try to be good. Even with these outward signs of righteousness, God may not know you and you may not know God. Remember, God looks at the heart.

A true financial miracle in today's society is to become alive with a willingness, an excitement, a determination, a decision, a purposefulness, and a drive to work. This thrust to work should be the normal temperament of us all, with the definition of *work* being an activity of betterment and productivity, using the skills we have for service to others.

According to another part of scripture from the prophet Zechariah, we are to execute true justice and show mercy and compassion. We are not to oppress the widow, the fatherless, the alien, or the poor (see Zec 7:8–11).

What is true justice? We are supposed to execute true justice even if we work the night shift at the local factory.

True justice seems like a fairy tale in most of the world, where kings, monarchs, tribal leaders, and cartels take what they want of your property, including your children, and kill those who do not submit. The crime may be that you are a Christian in a Muslim country. Is this true justice? If you doubt this assessment, visit Voice of the Martyrs for real stories of imprisonment, torture, and costly faith.

But our focus is on the financial miracles. One example is the relationship between employer and employee. Both sides have goals, priorities, and needs. True justice for the employee is being paid fairly, including some benefits such as health insurance, vacation time, and sick days. Imagine you are part of a family with children, and one child gets sick. True justice for the employee would be a merciful boss who allows employees to care for sick children, including paid time off to take the child to the doctor. Now consider true justice for the employer in the same situation. True justice for the employer would be for the employee to offer to make up lost time, especially to meet a production or delivery demand from a customer. For the boss to provide days off for family sickness is not a one-way street. It is a two-way street. The employee understands the employer's responsibility to customers and provides consideration to the boss by making up time or shows mercy to the employer by working through a temporary customer need.

UNEMPLOYMENT

America is blessed with unemployment compensation, which provides workers emergency funding to make it through bad times until new employment can be secured. During such a time, the focus of the worker is to secure new work. A worker may offer existing skills in a similar trade or older skills from past experience. A worker may even develop new skills or begin a business, selling something needed by others in the community.

During the hiring process, there is rejection, frustration, humiliation, and dissatisfaction. The human resources department investigates a worker's background, questions their skills, calls their references, and tests them in other ways. Much of the discussion seems one-sided, and it is very hard for those in the process to keep a positive attitude.

To help maintain a positive attitude and demonstrate to the rest of the family that we are a contributing member of the family, I suggest we insert home projects into our weekly schedules. A home project allows us to work with our hands and receive a sense of accomplishment and success. Our egos are restored after many days of rejection, and we again enjoy an accomplishment. Here are some ideas for projects. Painting is a great way to start, because everything can use a fresh coat of paint. Paint each room as an individual project, breaking down the work into no more than two-day projects. Your main work, remember, is to find a job. Finding a job includes a great amount of research, including visiting the local library, reading the papers from various cities, reaching out to local caseworkers, searching government websites, investigating training opportunities, and many other aspects of career choice.

Each room needs repairs and reconditioning. Cleaning, sorting, scrubbing, oiling, steam cleaning, and polishing are maintenance tasks that are often forgotten. Then there are types of work: window work, carpet work, wall work, curtain work, desk work, furniture work, garage work, machine work, lawn work, tree work, shrub work, roof work, shed work, auto work, and all of the projects contained therein.

Have you ever thought that God has deliberately put you at a crossroads in your career? Perhaps God wants to test you in all sorts of ways. Are you lazy and slothful, intent on getting as much money from welfare benefits, unemployment, and food stamps as possible? Do you intend to scam the system, lie about new employment, and work for cash under the table? Do you intend to feign a disability, attempting to qualify for a permanent disability payment?

Are you a person of integrity, understanding the financial miracle of support during this time of testing? Do you utilize your time to the utmost benefit, avoiding too much television, rabble rousing, and gang activity? Are you taking an education improvement class, reading trade publications, reading the Bible, and staying out of trouble?

During this time of testing, in order to keep your skills and attitude alert, you might consider volunteering. There are many places that need workers to care for animals, serve meals, gather clothing, repair cars, greet the downtrodden, and provide a smile and a glass of water to a stranger. Perhaps one of these many charities and churches will see your good efforts and hire you. Volunteering provides service to others, increases our serving skills, and provides spiritual growth, which is one element we need during this time of testing.

The proverbs of Solomon, the son of King David, have many short quips about work, the energetic, and the wicked. Here are some examples:

- A wise son makes a father glad.
- Treasures of wickedness profit nothing.
- The Lord will not allow the righteous soul to famish.
- The hand of the diligent makes wealth.
- He who sleeps in harvest is a son who causes shame.
- He who has a slack hand becomes poor.
- The memory of the righteous is blessed.
- The wise in heart will receive commands.
- A prating fool will fall. (See Pr 10:1–8.)

During a period of unemployment, consider reading the book of Proverbs to gain understanding.

V. Gilbert Beers writes about service and spiritual growth in a book on practical Christianity. He says our motive for serving God and others should never be what we will get out of it. If that becomes our motive, we are not giving with clean hearts, and God will not reward us with His full blessing. But if we serve because we want to give, we will get back much more than we give. We will grow in Christ and in our capacity to serve even more effectively.

Beers comments on the parable of the talents (a unit of money), which tells us much about the rewards for effective service (see Mt 25:14–30). The parable starts with the master of the house leaving on a long journey and giving each servant talents based on ability. The money was loaned to the servants. The servant given ten talents produced ten more. The servant given five talents produced five more. The servant given one talent buried the talent in the ground and returned it to the master when he came home. The faithless servant was given no reward. His unused talent was taken from him, and he was sent away from the presence of the master. But the faithful servants were rewarded—not with great riches to keep for themselves, but with greater opportunities to serve.

Beers says that a person with a serving heart appreciates this kind of reward. He or she realizes that service to our Lord and Master, Jesus Christ, is best rewarded with greater opportunities to serve. That is because through service, we grow spiritually and become larger vessels to carry His Word of life to those who need it.[6]

The talents represent all the skills and resources we have, including money, education, community resources like the library, government betterment programs, and innate attributes such as enthusiasm, faith, speech, determination, and positive attitude. I read a book once entitled *Enthusiasm Makes the Difference* by Dr. Norman Vincent Peale. He applied this philosophy in all types of situations and circumstances, demonstrating that individuals can succeed in tight spots and challenging environments with enthusiasm as a power and mover. Enthusiasm, the book's advertisers say, is the magic ingredient that can make the difference between success and failure. It can help you to improve your problem-solving abilities, overcome your fears, sharpen your mind, calm your tensions, build self-confidence, and kindle the powerful motivation that makes things happen.

As Christians, we should be filled with the Holy Spirit and do all for the glory of the Lord, as a response in thankfulness for Christ's love and sacrifice for each of us (see 1 Cor 10:31).

Christians may be frustrated with their current jobs and duties, thinking, "I can do better than this. I am more talented than they give me credit for. I have an education above this job. I have respect. This job is not meaningful. I want out." Even in Christian service, someone can be frustrated and feel his work is wasteful, not meaningful, and unsatisfactory.

I was teaching a Sunday school class. In an answer to a question, I said that God has placed each of us in varying positions in our homes, work, and communities. Start serving exactly where God has placed you. Search for people in need. Seek situations where comfort is needed. Seek God's direction. You will find God's power to move forward from your current position.

Later a man revealed to me that my comments had had an impact on him. The man was frustrated and thought of becoming a missionary in a foreign land, bringing people to Christ. Serving as a foreign missionary seemed more important and impactful than working a normal job. The man had not realized there are opportunities for building relationships and nudging people to Christ right where God has placed us.

A similar strategy is available for people in frustrating jobs. Start in your current situation and explore the depth of the job. Look into the products made and think of a better production process. Consider the resources used and find a better source of material. Imagine how to make the job more efficient. Similarly, explore the breadth of the job. Look into how the product is used and consider different uses and new sales applications. In other words, get into deeper waters with your job. The result will be a financial miracle. You will find new excitement in your work, which will be recognized and rewarded.

I talked to a contractor who said he was working long hours. "Why not hire some workers?" I asked. The contractor started a long description of the poor quality of available workers: they would not show up for work, would not follow instructions, and would complain about the weather. They caused him exhaustion each day. He said that one worker required repeated explanations of each procedure.

I see want ads in many storefronts, on flags in front of stores, on billboards, on electric advertising boards where product promotions used to be, and on television. The labor participation rate is less than 70 percent. How can people survive without work? There are plenty of opportunities for self-fulfillment and meaningful work.

I was a volunteer with the Red Cross organization during Hurricane Katrina. This was a massive hurricane that caused great damage in New Orleans because the city was built below the level of the lake nearby and the levee gave out. I was assigned in the accounting area for several weeks, keeping track of the disbursements to individuals for repairs. The maximum amount each person was eligible for was less than two thousand dollars, as I recall. When comparing addresses on some of the disbursements, one person discovered the addresses were in a local cemetery. A claimant needed an address in the disaster zip code to be eligible for reimbursement. Therefore people were stealing from the disaster funds by using the cemetery address. The natural disposition of people, the original tendency of their hearts, is to steal, lie, and cheat. Without a spiritual regeneration, all people are thieves and liars.

I was later transferred to a facility that provided food and shelter to those made homeless by the hurricane. There, I mopped the floors and cleaned. The room was filled with open cots. Each family's things were stored under their cots. The government had a strategy of purchasing trailers for some people to move into as alternative housing. One individual had a trailer waiting for him if he could pay fifty dollars to a taxicab to drive him there. He did not have money, so he stayed in the shelter, eating and sleeping there each day. Each day vendors and contractors would come to the facility and ask for workers for day wages. I asked the man why he did not take a day job and earn money for the taxicab. "Oh," he said, "I wouldn't want to do that!" Our nation has turned into a something-for-nothing society. The offer of a trailer could be considered a financial miracle, help in desperate need.

CHAPTER FOUR

FINANCIAL SUFFERING, PERSECUTION, AND JOY

FINANCIAL SUFFERING

There is suffering in the world. Each of us will physically suffer at some point and eventually die. There are similarities between physical suffering and financial suffering. In both cases there is pain, frustration, lack of energy, lack of hope, lack of motivation, guilt, depression, self-pity, and thoughts of suicide to end the suffering.

There are many forms of financial suffering. Not getting paid for work completed is financial suffering. At one time I was working for a local CPA firm and used my wages to pay my bills. It was early in my marriage. We were living on the edge, without money in the bank, so to speak. Then my paycheck from the CPA firm bounced causing a chain reaction. All my bill payments bounced, causing me frustration and problems with the vendors. What a mess. Apparently the bank where my boss did business had confiscated his checking balance to pay an outstanding debt without his knowledge. This is financial suffering.

If you are in business, financial suffering is not getting paid for the work you completed according to contract. I have stories of accounts receivable losses from men I considered honorable friends. In addition, getting paid late is financial suffering.

Legal tricks may be the cause of financial suffering, forcing you to pay for items beyond the scope of a project. At the end of a commercial lease, a landlord forced me to replace a furnace and air conditioning system that had been battered and duct-taped when we moved in. This was definitely heavy-handed, unjust enrichment to the landlord.

The government is the cause of financial suffering, requiring reports that take employee time. We suffer to satisfy IRS notices, complete census forms, and deal with government agencies that make up their own rules. The amount of paperwork imposed by agencies is onerous and oppressive.

For most of us, financial suffering is simply that we cannot seem to earn enough money from employment to pay our monthly expenses, even with great effort. We cannot keep up with constant repairs to car, home, and appliances, or manage medical expenses.

ADAM AND EVE

Adam and Eve lived in a perfect world without suffering. They had a loving relationship with God. But that was not enough for them. They sinned against God, ate from the tree of life, discovered the difference between good and evil, recognized they were naked, and broke the rules. The result was that rebellion became part of everyone's DNA. We are born with selfishness, self-love, stinginess, and self-centeredness. We become self-seeking, self-worshipping, self-serving, self-indulgent, self-absorbed, unthankful, ungrateful, unloving, and unkind. This list is the natural disposition of each person from birth.

It is easy to prove the natural disposition of humans by reading the newspaper. Each day there are murders, robberies, scandals, police actions, domestic violence, and all sorts of hateful actions. Our society is in a state of lawlessness, which is sin. There are drug wars, love triangles, drive-by shootings, corrupt politicians, false witnesses, smear campaigns, and worker slowdowns. There is looting after severe storms, during which household goods and retail stores are damaged. People think it is proper to steal anything, as if they have a right to steal when facing a catastrophe.

Without God as a restraint, threating an afterlife in hell, there is lawlessness, which is sin.

The Bible says that there is no one who is righteous, who seeks God, who does righteous works, and who understands the human condition (see Rom 3:10–12).

The general outcome from these human characteristics is physical and financial suffering, including personal, family, group, employment, social, and national suffering. God gave us rules of behavior called the Ten Commandments to give us a definition of sin. The Ten Commandments are not intended to save us, but to point out our sin. It is impossible to keep the intent of the Ten Commandments.

In order to have a government of the people governed for the people, there must be governing people with hearts willing to serve the people. Serving the people requires the governing people, the politicians, to abstain from accumulating personal benefits for themselves and their families. Politicians must have changed hearts that prioritize delivering justice for the people, for others. Since there is no one who does "good, not even one," a government of the people and for the people is an impossibility without a God who changes the heart.

There will always be suffering, pain, annoyance, distress, grief, sickness, sorrow, anxiety, damage, and loss concerning physical, mental, and financial attributes. People will blame God for their suffering and eventually call out to God for mercy when there is no other alternative for justice.

A HISTORY LESSON ABOUT SUFFERING

God desires to have a relationship with us, a relationship of trust, of conversation, of obedience, and of worship. God desires to bless us, make us holy, and show mercy when we are suffering.

Remember the saying that history repeats itself? We have a history written for us that explains God's reaction, which is punishment for disobedience and sin. The story is in the book of Judges in the Bible. The judges were not legal authorities or judicial decision-makers but spiritual and military leaders.

At Mt. Sinai, God made a sacred and binding agreement with the Israelites, called a covenant (see Ex 19:5–8). God's part was to make Israel a special nation, to protect them, and to give them unique blessings for following him. Israel's part was to love God and obey His laws. But because Israel rejected and disobeyed God, the agreement to protect them was no longer in effect. An angel of the Lord gave the Israelites a message.

The angel of the Lord reminded them that God had brought them out of slavery and out of Egypt through the desert. God had brought them into the land He had sworn to give to their ancestors, saying that He would never break His covenant with them. He instructed them not to make a covenant with the people of that land. But the Israelites disobeyed God and did not destroy the pagan altars. The angel then said that God would no longer drive out the land's prior inhabitants, and their gods would become snares to the Israelites (see Jgs 2:1–3).

Our gods have been a snare to us, trapping us in an endless quest for more money and power. We think that more stuff will at some point satisfy our desires and create freedom to do what we really want. The gods of wealth, power, name recognition, fame, and applause never satisfy.

The events of the period of the judges (about 320 years, from 1375 BC to 1055 BC) show that there was a cycle of events: sin-oppression-deliverance-death of the judge. The cycle repeats itself in a spiral downward of decay, corruption, violence, rancidity, and immoral disgrace. Are we returning to this decay and corruption? An elaboration of the cycle is found in the work of Tremper Longman III. There are five steps to the cycle. Perhaps the cycle of events is similar to your own life experience with step 3, crying out to the Lord for a financial miracle?

- Step 1: The children of Israel do evil in the eyes of the Lord (see Jgs 2:11; 3:7, 12; 4:1; 6:1; 10:6; 13:1).
- Step 2: Although the nature of this evil is rarely spelled out, their sin prompts the anger of God and results in oppression at the hands of some foreign nation (see Jgs 2:14; 3:8; 4:2; 10:9). The Israelites' sin was idolatry— worshipping Baal and the Ashtoreths (local male and female fertility/vegetation gods), forsaking the Lord, and remembering not the Lord or what He had done for Israel under Moses and Joshua.
- Step 3: During their oppression and defeat, the Israelites cry out to the Lord (see Jgs 3:9, 15; 6:6–7; 10:10).
- Step 4: The Lord hears their cry and raises up a deliverer, one of the judges (see Jgs 2:16; 3:9, 15; 10:1, 12). The deliverer is chosen and empowered by the Spirit of the Lord (see Jgs 3:10; 6:34; 11:29; 13:25; 14:6, 19).
- Step 5: Deliverance is often followed by submission of the enemy and a period of peace, during which the deliverer judges Israel, followed by the death and burial of the judge (see Jgs 3:10–11; 8:28–32; 10:2–5; 12:9–15).[1]

There are points and themes that apply to our lives and our nation. God changed His covenant agreement with Israel, the nation he chose to become his holy nation. His holy nation was intended to be an upright and righteous example to the surrounding nations, a nation of moral laws in the Ten Commandments. The Ten Commandments teach us to love God, to turn away from idols, to gladly hear His Word, to remember worship, to love one another, and to recognize sins of resistance to those in authority, including murder, adultery, false witness, stealing, and coveting.

God changed the covenant and changed His relationship to Israel. God allowed the Israelites to be defeated in battle and become oppressed. How could God allow bad things to happen to good people? Part of the answer to that question is that no one is good, not even one.

Our personal relationship to God may have changed through the years. Perhaps you were a church attender and believer in youth, but then succumbed to the religions of the world. Islam, Eastern religions, witchcraft, nature worship, new age practices, agnosticism, or secular humanism may have replaced God. Or perhaps you devoted yourself to the idols of work, business, sports, music, prestige, education, politics, science, power, sex, or money.

Has your relationship with God changed? Do you think that God is allowing your financial defeat and oppression because of your sin and disobedience?

Another point is that God desires for us to return to Him. God has mercy on us despite our unfaithfulness when we cry out to Him for mercy. "Judges leaves us with a paradox: God's relationship with Israel is at once both conditional and unconditional. He will not remove his favor, but Israel must live in obedience and faith to inherit the promise."[2]

God delivers His people using individuals He chooses— individuals who are not perfect but also are not involved with foreign gods, lust, doubt, and trickery. So there is hope for us today to be part of the great cloud of faithful witnesses filled with the Spirit of God.

A final point concerns repentance, which is explained in the footnotes of the Life Application Bible: "Decline, decay and defeat caused the people to cry out to God for help. They vowed to turn from idolatry and to turn to God for mercy and deliverance. When they repented, God delivered them."[3] The importance of this point is that "idolatry gains a foothold in our hearts when we make anything more important than God. We must identify modern idols in our hearts, renounce them, and turn to God for his love and mercy."[4]

ENVIRONMENT FOR A MIRACLE

It seems to me that if you desire a financial miracle from God, then you must first remove the negative actions that are preventing God from walking through your front door to chat with you. God wants to love and help us, but also desires fellowship, worship, humility, dependence, and reciprocal love, demonstrated by active service to others.

Once we begin to have a relationship with Jesus Christ and welcome Him into our hearts through Bible study, church attendance, forgiveness of sins, participation in Holy Communion, and prayer, we may think that our financial suffering will decrease. Pay raises will come, and life will be easier, with fewer disappointments.

But, surprise, the opposite may happen. "In fact, everyone who wants to live a godly life in Christ Jesus will be persecuted" (2 Tm 3:12 NIV). Our current sufferings, including financial suffering, cannot be compared to the glory we will receive in the resurrection in the last days.

When thinking more about the matter of an environment for a miracle, I am disquieted by the endless persecution of Christians throughout the world and through the centuries. Christians who refused to recant the name of Jesus Christ have been beaten and worse. They suffer and consider themselves joyful for the opportunity to suffer. Under communism, Nazism, Islamism, and other religions or sects, the persecution of Christians is widespread and vicious.

It is a reverse of normal thinking that a financial miracle may arrive under persecution more often than in an environment of holiness, prayer, and freedom to worship. The church becomes an underground church, meeting in hiding places, fields, and basements. The leaders are not wonderful speakers with doctorate degrees and expertise in homiletics, theology, Christology, transcendence, and eschatology, but people who have witnessed the fervent love of Christ with broken fingers and scars over their bodies.

How can Christians endure such torture? The Reverend Richard Wurmbrand has an answer in his book *Tortured for Christ*. Jesus spoke of Lazarus, a poor, oppressed beggar, dying and hungry, his wounds licked by dogs. In the end, angels took Lazarus to Abraham's bosom, where he received the glory and love of Jesus.[5] Wurmbrand mentions that he hates the communist system, but he loves the men; he hates the sin, but loves the sinner. Communists can kill Christians but communists cannot kill Christians' love toward even those who kill them. Wurmbrand says he does not have the slightest bitterness or resentment against the communists or his torturers.[6]

Wurmbrand says that the cruelty of atheism is hard to believe. When a man has no faith in the reward of good or the punishment of evil, there is no reason to be human. There is no restraint from the depths of evil that is in man. His communist torturers often said, "There is no god, no hereafter, no punishment for evil. We can do whatever we wish."[7]

Wurmbrand writes the following:

> God will judge us not for how much we endured, but how much we could love. The Christians who suffered for their faith in prisons could love. I am a witness that they could love God and men.
>
> The tortures and brutality continued without interruption. When I lost consciousness or became too dazed to give the torturers any further hopes of confession, I would be returned to my

cell. There I would lie untended and half dead, to regain a little strength so they could work on me again. Many died at this stage, but somehow my strength always managed to return. In the ensuing years, in several different prisons, they broke four vertebrae in my back, and many other bones. They carved me in a dozen places. They burned and cut eighteen holes in my body.... I should have been dead for years, I know myself that it is a miracle, God is a God of miracles.... I believe God performed this wonder so that you could hear my voice crying out on behalf of the Underground Church in persecuted countries.[8]

In *Tortured for Christ*, the editors included several letters about a girl, Varia. She was a member of a communist youth organization who was led to Christ by a woman named Maria. Maria visited Varia in a Russian prison.

When I saw her yesterday, she was thin, pale, beaten. Only the eyes shown with the peace of God and with an unearthly joy.

Yes, my dear ones, those who have not experienced the wonderful peace of Christ cannot understand it... But how happy are those who have this peace... For us who are in Christ no sufferings and frustrations should stop us...

I asked through the iron bars: "Varia don't you regret what you did?" "No," she answered. "And if they would free me, I would go again and would tell them about the great love of Christ. Don't think that I suffer. I am very glad that the Lord loves me so much and gives me the joy to endure for His name"[9]

Today in America, we do not experience physical torture or the need for an underground church. Our torture is a financial torture. Christians are denied jobs, denied benefits equal to those of non-Christians, and denied the ability to talk freely to peers about Christ. We are subject to harassment because we are pro-life. We are ridiculed for being religious, scorned for praying, and made fun of for not swearing.

Our response to those who persecute us should be to love our enemies, as Jesus Christ proclaims, but hate the sin. It is impossible to love the neighbor who persecutes you unless you receive a new heart, which gives you a totally different perspective on life. It gives you different expectations about money and what money accomplishes in your life. This change in perspective and expectations is what I call the "New Financial Nature".

Here are some of the things we can learn from persecution of Christians by governments under communism and Islamism. We can learn to endure financial hardships, standing firm in the belief that God loves us and wishes the best for us in the end. We can learn to persevere and resist influence by the government to quit working and receive benefits. We can resist politicians who vote to spend excessively, resist laws to abort the innocent unborn, and resist the pressure to accept dishonorable lifestyles. We can accept times that test our faith, dealing with them in the knowledge that God has given us abilities, energy, and brains to figure things out. We can seek out resources and refuse to give up. We can learn, with the power of the Holy Spirit, to love our enemies who fire us, give us bad jobs, refuse us sick days, deny us medical insurance, and overtax us.

Often our enemies are normal acquaintances but are influenced by Satan to do his bidding. We can learn the good news of Jesus Christ and the forgiveness of sin, resulting in a "New Financial Nature". We should show the world there is a new way to live. We can make examples of our lives, doing good unto others as we wish them to do unto us. We can learn that the struggle to the death, holding on to the hand of the Lord Jesus Christ, will lead to receiving incomprehensible love for eternity.

NATIONAL AFFLICTION

J. S. Feinberg says the Bible words referring to affliction seem to be used most often to refer to national affliction or trouble, rather than individual suffering. He uses the Egyptian bondage as a national example. The Israelites were held as slaves for four hundred years, crying to God for relief. God called Moses to approach Pharaoh and ask him to let God's people go. Moses performed wonders and miracles at the direction and with the powerful arm of God.

Another national example Feinberg gives is the calamity of the Babylonian captivity. Because of the Israelites' sins, God allowed the Babylonians to capture Jerusalem and export the citizens to Babylon as slaves, as a punishment for disobedience for seventy years. God punished his children as a loving father punishes his child, to teach obedience and respect.

Feinberg points out there will be national affliction during the last days, such as has not been since the beginning of the creation, nor ever shall be again.[10]

CORONAVIRUS

I can certainly interject a discussion of national suffering Americans endured, caused by the coronavirus. This included unemployment, medical cases, deaths, stay-at-home orders, diversion of production toward medical respirators and medical supplies, orders to stop air travel, orders to prohibit assemblies, cancellation of sporting events, home education requirements, and the collapse of the economy.

Further suffering resulted from the summer 2020 riots throughout America. These involved looting, arson, and the destruction of small businesses, all supported by the stand-down orders from city governments. That allowed the mass destruction of personal property, the abandonment of civil order, and the ruin of many lives. The thieves go free without punishment. It demonstrates a spiral into decadence, dysfunction, decay, and cowardice among mayors and governors.

It is as if the command of God to love your neighbor has no meaning, and our leaders have no memory of the Ten Commandments. This is a society that has turned to lawlessness and personal power, repeating the cycle of the biblical judges.

> In those days *there was* no king in Israel; everyone did *what was* right in his own eyes. (Jgs 17:6 NKJV)

> Whoever commits sin also commits lawlessness, and sin is lawlessness. (1 Jn 3:4 NKJV)

Mankind is not capable of personal restraint, kindness, and helpfulness. We are born in rebellion, with latent, unrestrained tendencies toward evil, sin, and self-centeredness. Only a miraculous outside power can change our evil nature.

PURPOSES FOR SUFFERING

Feinberg mentions that scripture is full of comments about the purposes of suffering. In regard to the unbeliever and the disobedient, he says scripture teaches that often God sends pain and affliction as a means of judgment for sin. And sometimes the individual or nation returns to the Lord.

1. In regard to why the righteous suffer, Feinberg mentions several reasons. Sometimes the believer will be afflicted as a means of chastisement (see Heb 12:5–7). The letter to the Hebrews says that we should not despise the chastening of

the Lord. To *chastise* means to scold, rebuke, and punish. Nor are we to be discouraged since a loving father corrects a son and attempts to move him in a new direction or change his motivation. In financial terms a rebuke is obvious when we get what we pay for, we end up with a debt that is hard to manage, we end up with a product that becomes worthless in a short amount of time, or we did not think a purchase through and it does not fit the intended purpose.

2. God uses affliction to keep His servants humble, as in the case of Paul (see 2 Cor 12:7). Paul had a thorn in the flesh, which was not clearly identified, and he prayed to have it removed several times. The prayers of Paul were answered. However, God's answer was that His grace was sufficient for Paul. Paul received the message that the thorn was intentional. It was meant to keep him humble, lest he be exalted above measure. We all have a thorn in the flesh. Perhaps we cannot speak in front of audiences. Perhaps we cannot understand current technology. Perhaps we have a defeatist attitude. Perhaps we have a load of cares about family. In all cases, we must learn to accept the disability and attempt to move forward with the skills we do have. I had an accounting partner who had a spouse and a child, both with kidney disease. He had to make many trips to the dialysis center each week, causing disruption in his productivity.

3. On some occasions, Feinberg says, the purpose of human affliction is to demonstrate to Satan that there are those who serve God because they love Him, not because it pays to do so (see Job 1-2). Job loved, honored, and worshipped God, and was very wealthy. Terrible tragedies happened suddenly in his life, including a windstorm that killed his sons and daughters, a raid on his oxen and donkeys that resulted in servants being killed, a fire that killed

sheep and servants, and another raid that killed yet more servants. All Job's possessions were gone, and his children were dead. In all this, Job did not sin nor charge God with wrong. Job says that the Lord gave and the Lord has taken away; blessed be the name of the Lord. It is my sincere hope that we will be so firm and committed in the Lord that when tragedy comes, as it surely will, we can move forward knowing God still loves us completely.

4. According to Peter, suffering promotes sanctification (see 1 Pt 4:1–2). The apostle Peter said that since Christ suffered for us in the flesh, we should have the same mindset to endure suffering for the sake of Christ and overcome the flesh. Sanctification is the process of God's grace by which the believer is separated from sin and overcomes lusts of the flesh. To be sanctified is to be set apart for God's purpose by the indwelling of the Holy Spirit. The sanctified person makes personal efforts to understand God's will, Word, and instruction. Sanctification is a lifelong process with times of setback, repentance, and renewal. We are to present ourselves as slaves of righteousness for holiness (see Rom 6:19).

5. Suffering refines the believer's faith (see 1 Pt 1:5–7). Refining uses fire to melt gold ore, which allows the unwanted minerals to be separated and removed. Refining the believer's faith uses suffering to remove the idols we cling to and trust, such as our title, our company, our education, our window office, and our investments. The worldly things we trust will disappoint, fail, and become worthless at some point. The suffering that takes place during financial losses will reveal the pure gold of faith in Jesus, a faith that will become stronger and more firm as the trials pass into the past. The lessons learned reveal who to honor and worship. Christ never fails us. He provides us with power to move forward, even after a total loss.

6. Suffering educates the believer in such Christian virtues as endurance and perseverance (see Rom 5:3–4, Jas 1:2–3). When we think of endurance, we visualize a prolonged hardship. This hardship is often a physical hardship, sometimes lasting a lifetime. Examples include blindness or lameness. Endurance turns into a way of life. Remember Joni Erickson Tada, who became disabled through a swimming accident? She was restricted to a wheelchair and needed help with brushing her teeth, eating, and performing all the personal tasks we take for granted. She used her wheelchair to provide encouragement to others as an author, artist, and radio host. She formed a charitable organization called Joni and Friends, an organization with a mission statement "To glorify God as we communicate the Gospel and mobilize the global church to evangelize, disciple, and serve people living with disabilities" [11] Another conception of endurance is as a positive force: "Oh give thanks to the Lord for He is good! For His mercy endures forever" (1 Chr 16:34 NKJV).

7. Suffering teaches the believer something more about the sovereignty of God, so that the believer understands the Lord better (see Job 42:2–4). God is totally sovereign and can accomplish anything He desires. His ways are not the ways of man. What we know about Him has been revealed to us through the Bible and through Jesus Christ, His Son. We do not know why there is suffering, but we understand that without suffering, we would not understand joy. Further, without suffering, we certainly would not pray for help.

8. Suffering gives the believer an opportunity to imitate Christ (see 1 Pt 3:17–18).[12] Peter in this passage says it is better to suffer for good than for evil. Jesus Christ suffered a hideous and dreadful death on the cross, receiving the

wrath of God for the punishment of the sins of the world. Jesus was put to death in the flesh but made alive in the Spirit. We suffer for doing good since we expose the sins and evil of the world, and the world takes revenge.

If any of these eight areas appear in the life of the believer, that appearance will be evidence of sanctification. Such sanctification is worked through affliction, Feinberg says.[13]

SANCTIFICATION

Sanctification is a lifelong process of being made holy, resulting in a changed lifestyle for the believer. The change covers all aspects of living, such as work, worship, relationships, love, service to others, and humility. All efforts are initiated for the glory of God. Sanctification is the work of the Holy Spirit, bringing one's whole nature under the influence of the new, gracious principles implanted in the soul. One's life is regenerated, becoming focused on service for others. Suffering is accepted without bitterness. Forgiveness for financial wrongs becomes easy when we realize unbelievers are under the influence of Satan.

Since sanctification changes all aspects of human nature, it changes financial references, including spending, saving, giving, purpose of money, and the results of work. This complete change of heart is what I call the "New Financial Nature".

In a passage from the book of Galatians, 5:22–24, the apostle Paul gives us the effects of regeneration in everyday living. He says the fruit or the visual change that results from the Spirit indwelling us is love, joy, peace, longsuffering, kindness, goodness, faithfulness, gentleness, and self-control. Individuals exhibiting these characteristics are Christ's. They have overcome the flesh, with its passions and desires.

The "New Financial Nature" includes financial love. How do you love someone financially? Financial love happens when others become more important on the priority list than oneself. Spending for others provides more satisfaction than spending for oneself.

What is financial joy? Financial joy is similar to the joy in heaven when one sinner repents and comes to Christ. Financial joy is found when all financial transactions are godly with no regrets.

What is financial peace? Financial peace has nothing to do with financial conflict or the absence of financial hate. Financial peace is the well-being received from peace with God and the overwhelming confidence that God provides.

What is financial longsuffering? Financial longsuffering is a patient endurance through financial struggles. It is not a resignation to adversity, nor is it a shrinking back. Financial longsuffering sees hope in the future. It understands that all suffering is temporary.

What is financial kindness? With the "New Financial Nature", financial kindness is quietness in response to financial mistakes made by the family. No longer do we become upset or stressed when financial accidents happen. We do not get angry with poor impulse control and foolish spending. We are kind and know that God provides.

What is financial goodness? Christians are saved to do good works. Financial goodness is a reaching out financially to help others in true need.

What is financial faithfulness? Faithfulness denotes trustworthiness and dependability. Financial faithfulness has two dimensions. The first is for Christians to become faithful stewards of the resources that God provides. The second is to understand that God is faithful in His provision and providence.

What is financial gentleness? Financial gentleness describes the communications we will demonstrate among family members when our hearts are changed to the Lord. We criticize with gentleness, always with the goal of restoring relationships.

What is financial self-control? Without the "New Financial Nature", financial control is a destructive force, providing power to the wage earner and humiliation to the rest of the family. With the "New Financial Nature", financial self-control allows for the family to receive higher financial priority. The heart changes, eliminating useless spending, showing discipline in paying bills, and supporting the church and charitable causes.

I took some time and space to describe how the Holy Spirit changes the financial aspects of family life. There are many marriages in which there are daily arguments concerning money and spending. The authority to spend is an important authority that can be shared.

I set up a saving account for my wife. Her name was on the account and her signature was authorized, but the account would transfer to me upon her death, preventing legal problems. She had authority to spend without accounting and without examination. The purpose was to provide her spending authority. She was a stay-at-home mom for many years.

I was told the story of how a marriage was destroyed. The man and sole breadwinner controlled the spending of his spouse by receiving notice from the bank whenever money left the account. This could happen when a debit card was used, for example. On one occasion his wife bought meals from a fast-food chain. She received a call from her husband, questioning why she had not made sack lunches for the kids instead of spending money. Purchases of clothing had to meet the husband's approval. The wife was homeschooling three children of her own and managing foster children as well. She did not have time to earn a separate paycheck.

The behavior of controlling the spending of a spouse with harsh words and actions is financial sin, exhibiting humiliation and anger.

CHAPTER FIVE

THE UNDESERVED FAVOR OF GOD AND FREEDOM

GRACE

We should start with a definition. According to *Holman Illustrated Bible Dictionary*, *grace* is undeserved acceptance and love received from another. Although the biblical words for grace are used in a variety of ways, the most characteristic use is to refer to an undeserved favor granted by a superior to an inferior. When used of divine grace toward mankind, *grace* refers to the undeserved favor of God in providing salvation for those deserving condemnation. In the more specific Christian sense, *grace* speaks of the saving activity of God, which is manifested in the gift of His Son to die in the place of sinners.[1]

Undeserved favor seems to be the thrust of the matter. What do you deserve, and what do you not deserve? This will be a startling statement for you: we deserve nothing but punishment and death. Our judge is God, the Holy of Holies, and we are sinners, failing to keep His laws and commandments. Thus we deserve to die for disobedience, unholy activities, and unholy thoughts. We are perpetual sinners without remedy.

In addition, God is a jealous God and wants our attention,

love, obedience, worship, gratefulness, and praise. Remember the Flood? Why did God bring punishment and death on the ancient people? The answer to this question is given in Genesis 6:5–8. God saw that the wickedness of man was very great, not only in actions and violence, but also in thoughts of evil. Every intention of men's hearts was to be evil continually. God was sorry He made man and was grieved in His heart. The society of the past sounds like the society of today, with wars, aggression, deceit, malice, and plots everywhere, including in the secret confines of the heart.

But Noah found grace in the eyes of the Lord. God promised not to destroy the earth and everything in it again with a flood. God gave us the rainbow as a testimony and visual reminder of this promise. Noah became the remnant. He continued as God's blessing for a new and different world. It was God's grace that allowed the world to continue, and it was sovereign grace that God selected Noah.

It was God's sovereignty that selected Abraham by grace to begin the journey to the forming of the nation of Israel, the nation that was to be a holy nation and an example to the world for holy and godly living. The nation of Israel failed to keep God's commandments and was punished by other nations. Eventually the Israelites were dragged to Babylon as punishment.

So it is by grace and mercy that each individual has possessions and is sustained by God, even though undeserving. Without grace, we would have nothing.

Compared to nothing, we have everything we need and in abundance. In the USA, we have much more than just clean water. Why does God allow this prosperity? The answer is grace, an undeserved benefit. And God allows this grace to the wicked as well as the righteous. However, there will be a judgment.

It seems to me that God will not provide a financial miracle just because we suddenly pray for help—just because we are at our wits' end with nowhere else to turn, thinking that God must show grace and mercy on our situation. Perhaps we should start with being thankful for the grace we have received. Perhaps when we look around at our possessions, our abilities, our connections, and our community, we will discover that by using our God-given gifts, we can actually make it. In other words, God has supplied everything we need, but we did not realize it and are too lazy to make use of what we have been given. Discovering our potential and available resources can be deemed to be a financial miracle.

Read the biographies of Christians who stood firm in battle, who were outcasts from society and yet persevered, prospered, and prepared the way for others to follow. These individuals were committed to God despite rough times. They worked through hardships and were able to discern financial miracles in their lives. I have personally experienced financial disasters and subsequent acts of mercy involving financial miracles. I desire for the reader to understand from my experience that financial miracles are a common truth.

For the Christian, the Lord's Prayer begins with "Our Father." The relationship God wants is a father-and-child relationship, a relationship of love. He desires to help us and has the full capability to sustain the earth. We become children of God through grace by faith. Once the faith relationship begins, we can ask God for those things for which we have a need in our particular calling. In the meantime, we are to serve others in love.

The scripture passage that is familiar is Ephesians 2:8–10. It says we are saved by the grace of God showing mercy on us. We appropriate this grace personally by faith—that is, we bring this grace into our lives and make it part of our being by faith. However, the faith we have is not from our own energy or effort. Faith is received from God as a gift. This is God's way of destroying boasting by religious individuals who say that the faith they have was created by their individual effort.

If we deserve nothing, then everything we have is by grace. The financial miracle is that we have property and freedom we have not worked for; others before us made the sacrifice.

Freedom in America is not freedom to riot, freedom to steal, freedom to form mobs, and freedom to destroy. It is the opposite: freedom to heal, freedom to bind up, freedom to build up, and freedom to take care of each other.

We will not receive a financial miracle until we begin a relationship with God through grace from Jesus Christ in love and obedience.

Remember the song "Amazing Grace"? Why was grace amazing to the author John Newton? John was a slave trader and participated in the inhumane treatment and death of many lives. The grace of God though forgiveness of sins is available to us. It will create in us a new nature of love and a "New Financial Nature". This is amazing grace, God's forgiveness, but also a new heart for those who believe.

Philip Melanchthon, in *The Augsburg Confession* issued in 1530, provides a definition of Christian perfection: "that we fear God honestly with our whole hearts, and yet have sincere confidence, faith, and trust that for Christ's sake we have a gracious, merciful God; that we may and should ask and pray God for those things of which we have need, and confidently expect help from Him in every affliction connected with our particular calling and station in life; and that meanwhile, we do good works for others and diligently attend to our calling."[2]

SET FREE

The grace of God through Jesus Christ by faith is truly amazing, undeserved, unbelievable, and remarkable. See, we are born in sin. Our actions and our thoughts are filled with sin. We think about exacting personal revenge for financial loss, receiving financial advantages, gaining prestige, changing laws to stymie competition, changing laws to make specific sins acceptable throughout America, and demanding personal power and control. We are slaves to sin. Sin controls us, and we are unaware of this tragedy in our lives until we come face to face with a holy God who terrorizes our conscience. Then we tremble, suddenly understanding our degeneration, depravity, and decadence.

The apostle John in his gospel reports Jesus as saying that anyone who commits sin is a slave to sin. Sin has a way of sticking with us. It is embedded in our lifestyle and our actions at the office, to the point where people recognize us, saying, "That is his way of doing business." We are slaves of sin or Satan and have a hard time breaking old habits, such as swearing, making crude jokes, cheating on taxes, and supporting companies that bribe us. We form caucuses and clans to perpetuate scandal and an ungodly way of thinking and acting. The only remedy is to receive a new heart, which suddenly exposes our decadence and decay. With new hearts, we can be unshackled and free from slavery to Satan.

Think of being a slave to a bad habit like smoking, which changes physical attributes. Smoking causes a restless, unsettled, anxious feeling to bubble up, turning to anger. One snaps at loved ones until the next smoke settles the nerves. A smoker is a slave to nicotine, which is sin, since the body is the temple of the Lord.

There are other examples in the physical world, like drugs, eating, and alcohol. The body does not have the capability to defend itself from these powerful influences. It is possible to be set free from these influences. The Alcoholic Anonymous program of the Twelve Steps is evidence of this possible freedom. Since the program is filled with references to God and His power, allow me to describe it in detail. Our goal is a "New Financial Nature" concerning money and financial miracles, with spiritual power abiding in the believer, setting the individual free from bad influences and changing the heart permanently with regeneration by the Holy Spirit.

THE NEW FINANCIAL NATURE

THE TWELVE STEPS

Where did the Twelve Steps originate? Bill Wilson and Dr. Bob Smith, the two men who founded Alcoholics Anonymous (AA) in 1935, drew their inspiration for the Twelve Steps from the Oxford Group, which advocated that all problems rooted in fear and selfishness could be changed through the power of God by following the Four Absolutes. The absolutes are a moral inventory of "absolute honesty, purity, unselfishness, and love."[3] Public sharing or confession was crucial. The Oxford Group also believed in the work of American psychologist William James, particularly his philosophy of pragmatism and the doctrine of the will to believe. That doctrine states that by changing the inner attitudes of our minds, we can change the outer aspects of our lives. The group was also influenced by William Silkworth, MD, one of the first medical professionals to characterize alcoholism as a disease.[4]

What are the Twelve Steps of Alcoholics Anonymous? The Twelve Steps are a set of guiding principles in addiction treatment that outline a course of action for tackling problems, including alcoholism, drug addiction, and compulsion. These are the twelve steps as provided by the Hazelden Betty Ford Foundation.

- Step 1: We admitted we were powerless over alcohol—that our lives had become unmanageable.
- Step 2: Came to believe that a Power greater than ourselves could restore us to sanity.
- Step 3: Made a decision to turn our will and our lives over to the care of God as we understood Him.
- Step 4: Made a searching and fearless moral inventory of ourselves.
- Step 5: Admitted to God, to ourselves, and to another human being the exact nature of our wrongs.
- Step 6: Were entirely ready to have God remove all these defects of character.

- Step 7: Humbly asked Him to remove our shortcomings.
- Step 8: Made a list of all people we had harmed, and became willing to make amends to them all.
- Step 9: Made direct amends to such people wherever possible, except when to do so would injure them or others.
- Step 10: Continued to take personal inventory, and when we were wrong, we promptly admitted it.
- Step 11: Sought through prayer and meditation to improve our conscious contact with God, as we understood Him, praying only for knowledge of His will for us and the power to carry that out.
- Step 12: Having had a spiritual awakening as the result of these steps, we tried to carry this message to alcoholics, and to practice these principles in all our affairs.[5]

Being set free in this way from a particular addiction certainly is a physical miracle, as long as one consistently follows the rules, attends the meetings, reviews the Twelve Steps, and uses deliberate and determined actions. Nevertheless, the desire to smoke, to drink, and to do drugs continues. Often there are relapses, because the human will is weak.

Our spiritual will is weak also, requiring an outside superpower to change our hearts and minds. But everything is possible with God through regeneration or conversion. Remember the words of the song "Amazing Grace": "I once was lost." I once was lost, doing everything correctly by the law but oblivious to the essence of sin. John Newton said that he was lost and then found and also that he was blind but now could see. He was referring to the sudden, dramatic awakening to the essence of sin.

The spiritual battle we face is not only against decisions we make in the world but against our own minds. The reason this is a true statement is that our power source is from God, using Jesus and the Holy Spirit to indwell the believer. This changes our outlook, changes our reaction to bad news, and changes our entire being: thoughts, language, work ethic, beliefs, goals, sacrifices, relationships, entertainments, priorities, spending, giving, saving, and suffering.

Ephesians 6:10–12 tells us about the power of God. Paul asks the congregation to be strong in the Lord and in the power of His might, using the illustration of a soldier putting on the armor of God. The armor of God may be physical armor for the soldier. For us, it is a mental and spiritual armor for fighting not physical forces but spiritual forces, which attack the mind and distort thinking and reasoning.

Satan is real, and his attack is on the mind, distorting our thinking with faulty excitement, imagination, pride, and lust. These attacks are defeated by Jesus Christ, who suffered the wrath of God for the sins of the world. God puts to death the attacks of Satan when we appropriate the Holy Spirit into our lives by faith.

The shackles that bind our ankles to the chain of sin can be destroyed, setting us free to a new power. Freedom provides us the joy of serving others, the strength of faithfulness, and the hope of salvation. God through Jesus Christ provides unending love and amazing grace.

We have a lot of lawn to mow. At one time I had two mowing tractors: one a fourteen-horsepower lawn tractor with a forty-two-inch blade, the other a forty-eight-inch, zero-turn, twenty-seven-horsepower tractor. I wanted to sell the fourteen HP tractor and was willing to give it to a friend at the church, who was having trouble maintaining his neighbor's lawn. I had just finished cleaning up the tractor—spraying off the grease from the engine, cleaning the grass from the wheels, checking the brakes and belts, and other procedures. It took many hours.

I told the church friend about it and put the tractor out at the end of the driveway with a price tag of $399. My friend from church did not come for it. However, my neighbor's son, who was a car mechanic with his own shop, happened to be at his father's home on that weekday. That was unusual. He came over and gave me four one-hundred-dollar bills. I thanked him for the one-dollar tip. The tractor was gone in about one hour.

Upon contemplation, this was obviously a financial miracle. Why was my neighbor's son there on an odd weekday, away from the repair garage of which he was the sole proprietor? Who carries four one-hundred-dollar bills in his wallet? Why didn't my friend from church pick the tractor up?

Praise the Lord.

CHAPTER SIX

MIRACLES ARE NOT FREE

THE COST OF MIRACLES

There is a cost to receive a miracle. The cost of a miracle is usually paid in terms of a changed attitude, a new understanding, a step out on a limb, patience, cooperation, submission, prayer, or repentance. Most people call out to the Lord when in financial pain and misery, acting like the Lord is a magic man required to provide a financial miracle just because they ask.

There is a cost to a miracle. One such miracle concerned the prophet Elijah. The background of his situation was a battle of the gods: Baal, the god of the Canaanites, versus the one true God. Baal was worshipped as the deity who provided fertility, rain, dew, and the growth of crops and animals.

The glossary in the book *What the Bible Is All About* provides us some detail about the god Baal. The name means "master." The category of *baal* (plural *baalim*) was used as the name of many false gods worshipped by the people of Canaan. They thought the baalim ruled their land, crops and animals. Eventually, Baal became the name for the chief male god of the Canaanites. They believed that Baal brought the sun and the rain and made the crops grow.[1]

The promoter of Baal worship was King Ahab of Israel, the northern kingdom of the Israelites. Ahab did more to provoke the Lord God of Israel to anger than all the kings of Israel before him (see 1 Kgs 16:33). The sins of the king were passed down to the people and made legitimate.

The story about the prophet Elijah is from 1 Kings 17:1-16. A prophet was a man called by God to deliver a message to the people. The prophet's word coming true confirmed that he spoke with the voice of God.

God was displeased with idolaters and Baal worship, so Elijah was sent to King Ahab to proclaim a drought. The drought would not end until God gave the message to Elijah to allow rain. Elijah hid by the Brook Cherith, which flows into the Jordan River. He received food from ravens. Eventually the brook dried up, and Elijah was instructed to go to the town of Zarephath and meet a widow.

The widow was there as God had said she would be, gathering sticks. Elijah asked her to bring him a little water in a cup and a morsel of bread. The widow responded that she did not have any bread, only a handful of flour and a little oil in a jar. She was in a desperate situation. She was ready to use the sticks to make a fire and prepare a last meal for herself and her son. Then she expected to die.

The prophet told her not to fear. He told her to do as she said, but first to make a small cake for him. To support his instruction, the prophet said that the word of the Lord God of Israel said that the bin of flour would not be used up nor the jar of oil run dry until the day the Lord sent rain on the earth. So the widow did as Elijah instructed, and they all ate for many days.

What are the costs to this miracle?

Elijah had to believe that the widow would follow God's instruction, reveal her situation, and reveal the elements available for a miracle. The jar of oil, the bin of flour, and faith were the elements. All miracles are created from physical, earthly elements and attached to faith.

John Walvood wrote, "The widow recognized Elijah as an Israelite and appealed to Yahweh in affirming that she had no bread; she had only a little flour and oil, enough for a last meal for her son and herself. Here was a Gentile woman in Phoenicia who believed in the Lord; she said she believed He is alive."[2]

The widow in obedience and faith had to use part of her last resources to make Elijah a cake first. She followed his instructions without complaint, providing for him before her child. What a cost this was! She was asked to use what she had to feed a stranger instead of her son. Would you use your last dollar to feed a priest?

Matthew Henry says that the person appointed to provide for Elijah—not a rich merchant, but a destitute, desolate widow—is commanded (that is, made both able and willing) to sustain him. It is God's way and His glory to make use of the weak and foolish things of the world and put honor upon them.[3]

The financial miracle you are waiting for may be accomplished with the help of a poor soul. He may give you a new product idea for your business if you will only recognize and speak to him from your lofty throne. The cost of the miracle is to lower your self-esteem, to humble yourself, to eliminate your I-can-do-it-myself attitude, to show respect to someone lower on the worldly ladder, and to seek God—which is not easy or appreciated in a liberal, godforsaken world.

The costs associated with our financial miracle will include using the resources available to us and having significant faith assurance that we and God together can get us through the current crisis. The resources available to us include tools, friends, former employers, the telephone, our time, our energy, and our faithfulness. Among the tools are the local library carrying newspapers from nearby cities, research on local businesses, special want ads listed in directories, the local unemployment caseworker, retraining classes, and your gumption, walking the streets and visiting businesses to hand out your résumé.

Back to Elijah. The battle was on. The Lord God of Israel

defeated the fertility god Baal with a drought lasting three and one-half years. Elijah was without food resources during most of this time. The financial miracle of provision was received by the widow.

YOUR GOD TODAY

Martin Luther asked, "What does it mean to have a god? Or what is God?"

"Answer: a god is whatever we look to for any good thing and for refuge in every need. To have a god is nothing else than trusting and believing in that deity from the heart. As I have often said, it is the trust and faith of the heart, nothing else, that make both God and an idol. If your faith and confidence are of the right kind, then your God is the true God. If, on the other hand, your trust is false, if it is misdirected, then you do not have the true God. For these two, faith and God, belong together. To whatever you give your heart and entrust your being, that, I say, is really your god."[4]

So where do you look for every good thing and for refuge in time of need? Does every good thing come from your skills? Your education? Your network? Your workplace? Your government? Your spouse? Your sports team? Your family? Your inheritance? Your club? Your department? Your president? Your bank account? Your portfolio? Your union? Your welfare payment? Your money? Your position?

All the items above are idols unless they are used for the glory of God and not for selfish purposes. When you start to live and serve the true God, only then will you be preparing for a financial miracle.

Miracles are available in your financial life. However, we need to have faith, to give up our rights to possessions, to surrender our stubbornness, to listen, and to allow God to use whatever we have for His glory.

You will find, as the Holy Spirit indwells you, that God may use you specifically to provide for a person in need, similar to the widow in the story of Elijah. You will be able to perceive and understand that God deliberately set you up in a situation to provide for someone's needs.

I worked in downtown Columbus, Ohio, for many years and crossed the grounds of the capitol building often. Because there were homeless in the area, I kept a five-dollar bill in my pocket in case I needed to help someone. One day I was crossing the state house common area and saw a person coming toward me. His face was scarred, with one eye damaged. He cupped his hands and lifted them beside my left shoulder. For some reason I reached my right hand into my right pocket, lifted my arm over my head, and dropped the money into his raised hands. It was as if God had dropped the money from heaven into his cupped hands as he looked up to the sky.

A TERRIFIED WOMAN

For some reason I worked later than usual one night in downtown Columbus. I packed up to walk one block south to the parking garage. The near sidewalk was closed. I crossed Third Street. On the east side of the street was the bus station, opened 24-7, with the usual shadowy crowd. There were single men, some military personnel, and mothers alone with children, staying for warmth and access to a restroom.

As I stepped onto the east sidewalk, a woman coming toward me made a left turn. I made a right turn, and we were walking shoulder to shoulder at the exact same pace. Neither of us said a word. We walked side by side for the half-block to the bus station entrance. There the sidewalk split to allow space for a car to drop off a passenger.

Once we ended up on the other side of the sidewalk, she exclaimed that she was terrified to walk alone past the bus station in the evening to get to the parking garage. She spoke about the dangers and her fears. She thanked me and thanked me for staying beside her. I said, without thinking, that I was happy to be her guardian angel. It was a miracle to her, and I felt I had been used by God.

The Holy Spirit can arrange meetings, situations, and circumstances to move us to the proper time and place. In addition, God seems to prefer to use people to accomplish His financial miracles. "Oh, please use me!" we should exclaim.

THE MISSING HANDLES

This is a personal example of a financial miracle. My daughter suggested we paint the kitchen cabinets and remove the drop ceiling and fluorescent lights. She and her two children have been living with me since her divorce, and it has been a joy to have them, especially since my wife died. She arranged for a painter, engaged an electrician, and selected a hanging light fixture. My job was to buy the cabinet handles, which I ordered for two hundred and fifty dollars. They were delivered before the project start date, and I left them in the box.

Upon opening the box, I discovered they were the wrong size. The screw holes were four inches apart instead of three inches. I had the packing slip and the credit card receipt, but I did not have the online purchase invoice. Without the purchase invoice, it was difficult to return items. From past experience, I knew I would suffer financial loss.

I pulled into the store parking lot and said a prayer that this would work out. When I offered the clerk the handles, he worked with the manager to locate the online order and accepted the return, giving me the full amount as credit. However, that manufacturer no longer made the three-inch handles I needed. The clerk suggested I look at what they had available.

As I walked down the aisle, the clerk pointed out a sale on

a discontinued handle. It had three-inch center holes and a brushed-nickel finish—exactly the color I needed. The design was acceptable, and the cost was seventy dollars.

I consider this a financial miracle. Perhaps you might say it was merely a series of coincidences. If you are interested in God and trust Him to work out personal dilemmas, you will be amazed at the resulting frequent miracles.

A FINANCIAL MIRACLE INVOLVING ELISHA

Elisha was a prophet who followed Elijah and was his understudy. This financial miracle involved a woman whose husband died, leaving debts and no assets. The creditor came looking for the family and threatened to commandeer the dead man's two sons to be his slaves.

The woman told Elisha about her situation. Elisha responded with two questions. He asked how he could help, and he asked what she had in the house. The woman replied that all she had was a jar of oil.

Elisha told her to borrow vessels from all the neighbors and to get many, not just a few. After she gathered the vessels, he instructed her to go into her house and shut the door. She was to take the oil she had and pour it into the borrowed vessels until they were all full. Then Elisha told her to sell some oil, pay the creditors, and live by selling the rest.

What was the cost of this miracle? The widow had to cry out to Elisha. It was probably a difficult task for a woman to approach a prophet. She had to confess the problem and admit to the debts, which are always a sign of overspending—a humiliation and a sign of mismanagement. Did Elisha just make the problem go away with a letter of bankruptcy or a magic production of cash? No. He asked what she had available. The miracle cost was to believe in the prophet and to follow instructions.

Instead of crying out to God to solve our financial problems,

I think we should look around for the items we have available. God has provided all we need, but often we do not see it, seek it, or recognize the possibilities. Perhaps we have available time, available skills, available imagination, available energy, or available tools. There are items available in our lives that we have not considered. With them, God can work a miracle.

The cost of a miracle includes our energy to stay the course, determination to see the project through, perseverance to continue working through ups and downs, faithfulness that God will provide insight, and prayer time to get in tune with God about the situation. Many ideas are generated from the inspiration of scripture and prayer.

The point is that in order for a financial miracle to occur in our situation, we must be part of the miracle. The miracle works through us; it does not happen to us.

Mortgage debt is not a crisis debt because one can always sell the house to pay off the mortgage and begin again with the remaining equity. A car loan can become a crisis debt when one needs a replacement car and has not paid off the old loan. Putting the balance of the old loan onto the loan for the new car increases the loan amount, sometimes creating a debt greater than the value of the new car. A third type of debt is consumer debt, generally credit card debt. Credit cards have very high interest rates, penalties for underpayment, and penalties for late payments. The goal should always be to pay off the balance of the credit card in full every month, even if you must sell something or suffer other consequences.

There was a family in debt. The father was determined to bring them out of debt. He gathered up the family and went from house to house in the neighborhood, asking for work. He offered to do mowing, cleaning, raking, shoveling—any odd jobs. He disclosed that the family was attempting to work themselves out of debt. The neighbors, upon hearing the story and seeing the good effort, often found work for the family.

CHAPTER SEVEN

EXPERIENCING MIRACLES FROM GOD

EXPERIENCING GOD

Have you ever experienced God?

I have experienced God working beside me in several situations. One type of experience is to deliberately set yourself up for a task beyond your capability. You will see God's help in action. In this case, as the scripture says, God's power is made perfect in weakness. When we are weak, God is strong.

It takes prayer and deliberation to understand God's will for you to move forward. Going into the ministry, preparing for seminary, starting a business, traveling overseas on a humanitarian mission, and many other situations require hearing God's call and preparing to sacrifice. Sometimes it is difficult to determine if the calling is really personal ambition and pride or God's purpose for your work.

SELF-EMPLOYMENT

I was a member of an accounting firm in Columbus, Ohio, which included the sons of the retired older principals. The sons had liberal ideas about the management of the firm, in conflict with my ideas. At the same time, I was increasing my study of scripture. I grew increasingly uncomfortable with the ideas of the younger principals.

At some point, the reader may experience the same frustration and uneasiness in their employment. Perhaps it may be due to fraud in marketing, unfairness in administration, dishonesty in handling customers, internal politics, or many other issues. These events may be the Holy Spirit prodding you to move on. If you find yourself in this situation, be sure the prodding is based on God's calling and not selfish ambition, greed, or ego.

I was called by the Holy Spirit, who made me unsettled, unfixed, disconcerted, uncomfortable, and eager to leave the firm. I was justified by Malachi 3:10. This scripture passage is often use by stewardship committees because it asks for the congregation to bring into God's temple a tithe. A tithe is 10 percent of the giver's income. The passage says this is a test of God. If one tithes, then God will bless that person, and the blessings will be in abundance.

This is an Old Testament passage. The law said if one was obedient, the result would be blessing, and if one was disobedient, the result would be a curse. The Bible Knowledge Commentary reads: "One must be careful in applying these promises to believers today. The Mosaic Covenant, with its promises of material blessings to Israel for her obedience, is no longer in force (Eph 2:14-15; Rom 10:4; Heb 8:13). However, the New Testament speaks about generosity and giving. While not requiring a tithe of believers today, the New Testament does speak of God's blessing on those who give generously to the needs of the church and especially to those who labor in the Word (Ac 4:31-35; 2 Cor 9:6-12; Gal 6:6; Phil 4:14-19)."[1]

I should go back several years and describe how I came to depend on the Lord for such a leap of faith as starting my own accounting firm. This was mostly the result of me taking a two-year course called *Crossways: A Survey Course of the Narrative and Major Themes of the Old and New Testaments*, published by Parish Leadership Seminars in 1979. The notebook included drawings of many books of the Bible, charts of many themes of the Bible, lists of information, and tests.

The leap of faith occurred on December 15, 1992, when I started my accounting firm without clients from my old firm, since I was under a non-compete agreement. I definitely was under stress those first months, without income, my savings being eaten away by everyday expenses.

In February 1993, God sent me a monthly client. It was an audit client I had worked for years before, which had been purchased by a foreign company that needed controllership services, including monthly financial statements. One unusual item was that the president needed a place to host dinner and introductions in a private, high-class setting in downtown Columbus. At the time I happened to be a member of the University Club of Columbus, which was a perfect venue. Clearly this opportunity was designed by God. The University Club membership was too expensive for me to continue, but it was available when God needed it.

This was a financial miracle, because I was struggling with a mortgage and three small children. God has sustained me many years, from the start of my business through non-Hodgkin's lymphoma, chemotherapy, a bone marrow transplant, the failure of a gymnastics business partly owned by my wife, polyneuropathy, early retirement due to ill health, and the death of my wife. I continue to trust Him. "Blessed *is* that man who makes the LORD his trust" (Ps 40:4 NKJV).

TRAGEDY AVOIDED

Another type of experience with God is the tragedy-avoided experience. God suddenly shows up and intervenes to prevent death or disaster. God literally saves us.

I was a young partner in an old, established accounting firm in Columbus, Ohio. That story is itself a financial miracle, but not part of this story. One of my partners had a teenage son who was killed in a traffic accident at the intersection of State Route 62 and Interstate 270, which is the outer belt around Columbus on the south side. Many months after the accident, I was entering this same intersection, driving down the ramp to a traffic light. I stopped at the light.

I was driving an American Motors Matador, which had a very fast-to-the-touch accelerator that caused the car to leap at the start. I was thinking about my partner's son who had died at the intersection. Then the light turned green.

I started into the intersection. For some reason, this rabbit of a car stopped halfway into the intersection, in front of two lanes of cars heading north on Route 62. It must have seemed odd to the cars behind me, but no horns sounded. All seemed still and quiet for perhaps ten seconds, although the time could have been longer.

Then a car flew by directly in front of me, traveling at about forty miles per hour. The car had run the red light in its lane of travel. It had swerved around a car that was properly stopped, missing my car by ten feet or so. The driver was shaken and immediately pulled off the road.

This was clearly a miracle, and it saved my life. My heart pounds just thinking about God's intervention and mercy.

ANSWERED PRAYER

A third type of experience with God is through answered prayer. We have a five-acre lot divided between about two acres of lawn and three acres of field, with plenty of trees. I was mowing the property one day, when the zero-turn mower suddenly would not engage its blades. The problem appeared to be the PTO starter switch.

So I contacted my internet-friendly parts company, and within a week the part arrived. The grass continued growing. The PTO switch did not help, which was thirty-six dollars down the drain. I contacted a tractor repair company. They wanted seventy dollars to haul the tractor into the shop for the repair.

The lawn and field continue to grow. At this point I was praying for a mow. The tractor repair company told me to look for a bracket in the lawn, which was needed to install a new clutch. I tried with no success.

It had been approximately three weeks. I wanted to go out of town on Thursday and stay for the weekend. The mowing really needed to be accomplished. Wednesday was the deadline, since it takes three hours to mow the lawn and another three hours for the field. Lord, what could I do?

I called my neighbor, who was not home. I left a message asking him to allow me to borrow his tractor. There was no call back. I called my other neighbor and left another message. No call back. I called a third neighbor, who is a Christian, and he said he had just got back into town. If I had called the day before, he would not have answered.

This neighbor let me use his zero-turn tractor, which had a sixty-inch mowing path, after he finished mowing his own lawn. I mowed my lawn to four inches and the field to five inches to not leave too many clippings. Even so, there was a furrow of mower clippings on the field. It looked like a farmer's field after harvesting straw. I finished in record time and returned the mower at about seven thirty that evening. God provides.

I have had a number of experiences with answered prayer. Part of the key to effective prayer is to be specific. Ask God for what you specifically need to help with your God-directed tasks.

I remember camping in a pop-up camper with young kids and a wife who had made the rule that camping did not involve tents. We used a cooler for our food that operated on a motor. The motor could connect to a cigarette-lighter outlet or, after we parked, a direct current converter. It was a special converter designed only for this type of cooler. The converter went bad and failed. I prayed for a replacement and anxiously went to a store, hoping it was inexpensive. And there it was, sitting on the bottom shelf all alone, with a "Discontinued" sign on it and a large markdown. God provides.

John 15:5–8 discusses the unity of the Christian with the Father. It uses the image of a vine and the branches: God is the vine, and Christians are the branches. Sap and nutrition come from the vine, such that the vine abides in the branch and the branch abides in the vine. With both abiding in each other, they yield much fruit. But without the vine, we can do nothing. If we do not abide in the vine, we are cast out and thrown into the fire. On the other hand, if we abide in the Father, and the Father's words abide in us, we can ask for what we desire, and it shall be done for us.

If you desire a financial miracle from God, then you will need to become a branch of the vine and abide in Jesus. You will need to walk with the Lord through thick and thin, despite all obstacles or adversities—a walk that will continue regardless of circumstances.

To abide in Jesus means to stay, to continue, to remain stable, to endure, to submit, to put up with, to withstand the consequences, to suffer for and hang tough with Jesus, the Son of God. He loves you, desires to receive you in heaven, and desires you to honor Him for His Father's glory.

The financial miracles you receive are to honor and glorify Jesus and the Father. Yes, we receive the benefit. But the process of the miracle unfolding— the elements connecting with such perfect timing, the interaction of people who are mostly unaware they are being used—is remarkable and clearly an act of providence.

Perhaps you have been involved in a close call, a series of incidents, a dramatic turn of events, a lucky time, a wish come true, a remarkable support, or a time of mercy. If one walks close to the Lord with intention, accepting the ridicule of people who make fun, then one will start to see the miracles that take place close by. One will begin intentionally to wait and see what God will do to help in a stressful situation and, eventually, to wait with some excitement.

PAUL

Under the heading of "experiencing God," I would be remiss if I did not discuss the trials and miracles of Paul, the apostle called by God from being a persecutor of the church to a supporter and determined missionary. Paul was sent to preach the gospel of Jesus Christ throughout the region of modern-day Turkey, Syria, Greece, Macedonia, Israel, Cyprus, Lebanon, and Italy. Because he had persecuted the church, he considered himself the worst of the apostles. He was amazed at the grace of God, who used him to bring the good news to the Gentiles.

If you think that you are not worthy to become a leader in the church and bring the news of forgiveness to the people, then think again. Look at the evidence. Abraham was deceitful and said his beautiful wife was his sister to avoid being killed by tribesmen. Yet Abraham was chosen by God to become the founder of the nation of Israel. Moses committed murder and fled into the desert to escape reprisal. Yet Moses became a messenger of God and confronted Pharaoh with the demand to let God's people go. King David committed adultery and indirectly murdered the wronged husband. Yet God used King David in the lineage of Jesus. It was said that David was a man after God's own heart (see Acts 13:22). John Newton was a slave trader, involved in the deaths of many innocent men and women. Yet God used John Newton as a pastor and writer of the song "Amazing Grace". Charles "Chuck" Colson went to prison for Watergate-related crimes. Yet God used Chuck to found the Prison Fellowship.

When we become in tune with God through Jesus Christ, God will send the Holy Spirit to indwell us, giving us the power to say no, take risks, confront fraud, vote for moral laws, leave the gang, discern deceitful news, and receive direction in making decisions.

Here is an example of Paul finding his way with the help of the Holy Spirit. These events are found in Acts 16:6–10. Paul and Timothy had traveled through Phrygia and the region of Galatia, which are in Turkey today. Since they were on a missionary journey, they had flexibility in which way they should go. They were independent of direction from the church in Jerusalem. Scripture says that they were forbidden by the Holy Spirit to preach the word in Asia. This may have been a direct revelation through a dream. Paul and Timothy went to Mysia and tried to go into Bithynia, but the Spirit did not permit them. The direction from the Spirit may have come in the form of circumstances, a word of prophecy, a vision, or some other prompting. Finally, one night Paul had a vision in a dream. He saw a man from Macedonia asking him to come to Macedonia and help. Thus the direction of the missionary journey became clear by way of a call from the Holy Spirit.

I am suggesting that you may receive a message from the Holy Spirit, calling you to move to a new vocation, a new employer, or a new leadership position. The Holy Spirit may call upon you to make a decision about financial matters. The Holy Spirit is involved in all matters of life. The Holy Spirit can make you unsettled about your circumstances and desire change. The Holy Spirit uses conversations, books, sermons, dreams, stories, and many other ways to prod you into following a different path.

In the fall of 2008, I was diagnosed with non-Hodgkin's lymphoma and started chemotherapy treatments. Was God asking me to retire? The treatments helped, and I was in remission for a while.

In the fall of 2010, I was well enough to qualify for a bone marrow transplant. My sister was qualified to be the donor. Was God asking me to retire? I was in remission and considered cured except for the host-versus-graft disease. My body was rejecting the new blood being produced by my sister's stem cells. My blood type changed to my sister's blood type. Was God asking me to retire?

In May 2015, I had a transfusion as part of my treatment routine. I felt a tingling. The tingling got worse throughout my body, to the point that when I held hands with my wife, she could sense the tingling. It was polyneuropathy. I underwent various tests at several hospitals, with no relief or treatment plan.

On October 16, 2015, the day after the filing extension deadline for income taxes, I was told that a neurologist appointment was not available for three months. Could I make it through year-end tax deadlines with no relief? Was God asking me to retire?

Finally, the Holy Spirit called me into retirement, saying God would provide and not to be anxious about the matter. Looking back, I can say it was a favorable decision and a life-changer. I felt uncomfortable enough with this unknown disease that I was going to let God have His way with me. During the next two years. I researched and completed the book *Financial Sin and the New Financial Nature*.

Financial miracles are generally positive. However, avoiding financial disasters has the same effect. Which is better, increasing income or decreasing expenses? Both have the same effect on net income. Many people would say a reduced footprint, a simpler lifestyle, a less stressful occupation, a safer work style, and a greater family involvement are better choices than maximizing revenue.

God is for you. He is on your side. He loves you. He wants you to depend on Him. He wants to be your God. He wants to get close to you.

SINGING IN PRISON

Paul and Silas were in the city of Philippi in Macedonia when they met a slave girl who predicted the future for her owners, by means of a spirit that possessed her. Paul became so disturbed by her that he called out in the name of Jesus Christ for the spirit to come out of her. It did. The owner, realizing he would lose income, stirred up the crowd against Paul and Silas. These events are recorded in Acts 16:22–31.

The crowd reacted. The magistrates became convinced of their wrongdoing and had them beaten with rods and thrown into prison. The guard put them in the inner prison and fastened their feet in stocks.

About midnight, scripture says that Paul and Silas were praying and singing. The other prisoners were listening. Apparently the Holy Spirit was listening also, because suddenly there was an earthquake. It shook the foundations of the prison and opened the prison doors. Everyone's chains were loosened.

The prison guard awoke and was about to kill himself, supposing all the prisoners had escaped. Paul called out that they were all there. The guard rushed in with lights and brought them out, asking, "Sirs, what must I do to be saved?" (Acts 16:30 NKJV).

They answered him that in order to be saved, one must believe on the Lord Jesus Christ (see Acts 16:31).

There are numerous miracles in this passage. Paul and Silas did not die from the beating. They experience joy strong enough to inspire song and prayer in prison. The earthquake opened the prison doors. Their chains fell off. No prisoners escaped. Paul saved the life of the guard.

With Jesus as your trust, you will be able to pray and sing in your financial prison—a prison from which there may be no way out. You may have no mobility to go to another community, no relief from ill financial treatment, or no apparent financial opportunities. Nevertheless, the miracles of God to Paul and Silas in prison should provide hope. If we stop focusing on inward feelings of defeatism, we can instead focus on finding a way to serve others, using our God-given talents. There is always hope, because our ultimate goal in life is eternity in heaven, where there is unending love.

God loves us through our circumstances and in spite of our circumstances. The love of Jesus is above our circumstances, pointing us away from our current financial prison to the hope of the resurrection and the heavenly banquet. I once had a dream about a heavenly banquet. The long banquet tables held no food, but there was laughter, singing, smiles, and friendship.

CHAPTER EIGHT

FINANCIAL HOPE AND A NEW HEART

FINANCIAL HOPE

The word *hope*, according the Webster's Dictionary, is a desire for some good, accompanied with an expectation of obtaining it, or a belief that it is obtainable. Hope in the Bible is a confident expectancy because it is based on facts and not wishful thinking. These facts are understood and have been experienced by the Christian who is connected to God through Jesus. It is a shared expectation, because Christians fellowship together and read about others in stories and testimonies from ages past. On this firm basis, the Christian has a confident expectation for the future.

God loves everyone, without exception. God desires to be our personal God. He desires for us to be His personal family, His treasured possession, and His holy nation. Being connected to Him and His will for us, we trust Him with our hopes secure.

Are you part of His holy nation? Do you depend on Him? Are you excited about each new day, waiting with confident expectation for the good that Jesus has in store for you?

The religious leaders of Jesus's day were waiting and hoping for a Messiah who would save the people Israel. Their idea of a Messiah was a mighty ruler who would defeat the Romans and bring back the prosperity of King David. The people would flourish, becoming wealthy, and the Jewish rulers would rise in prominence and fame.

The Messiah came. And what the people saw and heard was different from what their religious rulers expected. Most did not understand the message. The message is not understood today.

The mission of John the Baptist was to announce the coming of the Messiah and make His way straight. The dilemma John the Baptist found himself in is described in the gospel of Matthew 11:2–5. Things were going well for John. The people were being baptized for the forgiveness of sins. When confronted by the religious leaders about his authority, John called them a brood of vipers. He asked them who had told them about the coming wrath of God and judgment.

Soon John found himself in prison. He questioned whether the Messiah was coming to overcome wickedness, judge sin, and bring in His kingdom. If so, why was he in prison?

We can ask a similar question. If I am a practicing Christian, whom God loves, and have the power of the Holy Spirit indwelling in me, then why am I suffering? Why are things not going so well?

John, doubting and confused, sent two of his disciples to ask Jesus if He was the Messiah or whether another should be expected. Jesus instructed those disciples to take note of the things they saw and heard, including the facts that the blind saw, the deaf heard, the lame walked, the dead were raised, and the poor were having the gospel preached to them.

Can you imagine being blind and groping around to find your way—unable to enjoy the beauty of spring flowers, unable to understand immense mountain structures, and unable to contemplate the vast universe of stars and planets? To have one's eyes opened is a miracle with many financial implications. It is a miracle of freedom to run without stumbling, to catch and throw, to look into the eyes of one's beloved, and to get close to God by reading the Bible, attending worship, and glorifying Him through engagement with nature.

We can complete a similar analysis with each of the physical miracles: the lame walk, the lepers are cleansed, the deaf hear, and the dead are raised up. Each physical miracle creates a new freedom, a new opportunity, a bright future, a changed attitude, a new hope, and a new way forward, without the shackles and stigma of a disability. It is a life-changer that includes financial implications.

Jesus says that a similar life-changing experience happens when the poor have the gospel preached to them. The underlying assumption is that the poor are unloved because the poor have few assets that are connected to and understood to be blessings from God. In the absence of physical blessings, the interpretation goes, we have evidence that God does not love the poor. The rich have God's blessings and love; the poor do not. More possessions equal more of God's love. Few possessions mean less of God's love.

The true message is that God loves everyone equally. He gives everyone the same hope, which is the hope not of receiving more possessions, but of receiving everlasting life. The poor as well as the rich can hope for eternity in heaven, where there are no tears, no heartaches, no depression, and no struggle. Instead, there is joy, singing, friendship, and love. This is a message for the soul, the attitude, the personality, and for the mind. It creates satisfaction, hope, love of the earth, and love of friends, regardless of our circumstances. This hope pays no attention to our possessions. It separates our possessions from the joy of knowing Christ. The response is one of freedom from being put down. Yes, I may have few possessions, but God loves me anyway. God sent His Son, Jesus, to take my sins upon the cross and die for me. I can stand up in the midst of my poverty and be useful to Jesus, regardless of my financial circumstances. I can shout for joy with a mind of positivity, refreshment, renewal, and hope.

Please understand that we can always be useful, helpful,

compassionate, loving, kind, and able to work to bring the kingdom of God to others we come in contact with each day. God needs our help. He wants to be our God, and for us to be His people.

After thinking about Jesus and understanding who He is, we are suddenly terrified, realizing our sinfulness and depravity. Sin calls for our repentance. We seek forgiveness and request a new life in Christ. A miracle takes place. We receive the Holy Spirit by faith, which is the third Person in the Trinity (Father, Son, and Holy Spirit). The Holy Spirit gives us a new heart—not an amended heart, but a new heart.

> I will give you a new heart and put a new spirit within you; I will take the heart of stone out of your flesh and give you a heart of flesh (Ez 36:26 NKJV).

> Jesus answered and said to him, "Most assuredly, I say to you, unless one is born again, he cannot see the kingdom of God" (Jn 3:3 NKJV).

The concept of a new heart is genius and incredible. Remember that God said, back before the Flood, that man's heart is inclined to evil continually, without remedy. God was sorry He made man. The remedy for an evil heart is not to do good works, which do nothing for the heart, only giving the person self-pride. Giving money to put your name on a building does nothing for the heart; it only exhibits personal glory. But providing a person with a new heart will change everything. Imagine an elaborate picture of you on the wall, showing all your personal feelings, activities, and relationships. If you have an old heart, the picture is crooked, with everything out of balance and in disarray. A new heart straightens the picture, with all relationships in proper order and emphasis.

With the Holy Spirit, we have the power to withstand tribulations, accept losses, and forgive without discussion, all the while knowing that God will provide for us. There is an unnatural power with the Holy Spirit, giving strength to the mind to interpret events in a totally different way. Being laid off from work becomes an opportunity to use skills elsewhere; it is not a devastation. There is always hope for the future.

LOSS BECOMES BENEFIT

At one time my accounting firm lost its biggest client after I completed their tax return, which showed a loss for the year. This organization was entitled to carry back a loss to earlier years, which resulted in a large refund being owed to them. I said I would complete the refund carryback after my fees were paid.

In order for the organization's new accounting firm to complete the refund, they requested certain records. We had an in-person meeting, during which they paid my fees and I provided my copies of those records. Please note that the organization's original documents were always in their own files. As a Christian, I was not bitter about the loss. These things happen, and God will provide. Financial losses are to be expected.

Christ said that we would be persecuted. Today Christians are persecuted terribly in Middle Eastern countries. In the United States, governments and their agencies suppress conservatives, causing great financial loss to those defending themselves. Christians should wait, pray, and persevere during these times, because God will provide justice. We can take comfort that there are many passages of scripture that indicate the Lord will provide justice for the oppressed (see Ps 103:6), maintain the cause of the afflicted (see Ps 140:12), and justice for man comes from the Lord (see Pr 29:26). There is no other God; He is a just God and Savior (see Is 45:21). Morning by morning, He dispenses justice (see Zep 3:5). Masters, provide your slaves what is right and fair (see Col 4:1).

Let's return to my story about the lost accounting client. My invoice was paid, the company received my copies of their records, and I went about my business. Several months after this incident, I read in the newspaper that the company had gone bankrupt. I now understood why I had been moved away from my largest client—I was being saved from an entanglement in bankruptcy. I was being saved from further loss of income. I was being saved from wasted time. Glory be to God. This was a financial miracle.

Being scammed becomes an opportunity for learning and a chance to warn others. This happens with decreased bitterness with the "New Financial Nature". Witnessing corruption in government, we are empowered to stand up, knowing God will provide despite the attempts of the government to use various agencies to suppress us.

TRIBULATIONS

The apostle Paul, in an important scripture passage, says that practicing Christians glory in tribulations, knowing that tribulation produces perseverance and perseverance produces character. In character, we find hope (see Rom 5:3). When we are in financial distress, Paul says we can have confidence in hope, because the Holy Spirit has been poured out in our hearts.

The Holy Scripture, the Bible, speaks to the poor, the fatherless, and the widows collectively through both the Old and the New Testaments, speaking of mercy, justice, and benevolence. There are many passages that give us hope.

> [Jesus said,] "The Spirit of the LORD is upon Me, Because He has anointed Me To preach the gospel to the poor; He has sent Me to heal the brokenhearted, To proclaim liberty to the captives And recovery of sight to the blind, To set at

liberty those who are oppressed; To proclaim the acceptable year of the LORD" (Lk 4:18–19 NKJV).

Liberty to the captives and the oppressed includes those who are financially captive and financially oppressed by low wages, required overtime, poor working conditions, lack of benefits, and oppressive government rules. The liberty we receive is liberty of the soul, attitude, and mind, knowing that God will provide in marvelous, unusual, and unexpected ways. We may not receive higher wages, but somehow—and this is a financial miracle—we will become satisfied and fulfilled with what we have.

At one point during one of the stewardship programs at church, a lady and I were discussing the tithe and giving. If I recall, the woman said (I think she was a single mother) that she had leaped into tithing, and she felt less financial stress than before. How could that happen? She said that her financial priorities suddenly changed. Purchases that had seemed important before were no longer important. She was satisfied. This is an incredible financial miracle.

When I first started in self-employment, my income was greatly reduced. But a financial miracle was in the making. My wife's job moved from part-time to full-time, and then she earned additional income from providing training services for her employer. When our mortgage became a burden, miraculously my father offered to refinance my home mortgage so he could receive a higher yield on his investments. He even increased the principal so that we received additional cash. Amazingly, God provides. These are financial miracles.

ELIZABETH AND MARY

Elizabeth, the wife of Zacharias, was pregnant with John the Baptist when she met with Mary, pregnant with Jesus Christ by the Holy Spirit, in the gospel of Luke (see 1:39–55). John the Baptist was to make straight the path for the coming of the Messiah, as one crying in the wilderness. John the Baptist was born first.

Mary went into the hill country and entered the house of Zacharias, where she greeted Elizabeth. When Elizabeth heard the greeting, the babe leaped in her womb. Elizabeth was filled with the Holy Spirit and called Mary blessed among women, and the fruit of her womb blessed also.

Mary responded with humility, thankfulness, and insight.

> And Mary said: "My soul magnifies the Lord, And my spirit has rejoiced in God my Savior. For He has regarded the lowly state of His maidservant; For behold, henceforth all generations will call me blessed. For He who is mighty has done great things for me, And holy *is* His name. And His mercy *is* on those who fear Him From generation to generation. He has shown strength with His arm; He has scattered *the* proud in the imagination of their hearts. He has put down the mighty from *their* thrones, And exalted *the* lowly. He has filled *the* hungry with good things, And *the* rich He has sent away empty. He has helped His servant Israel, In remembrance of *His* mercy, As He spoke to our fathers, To Abraham and to his seed forever" (Luke 1:46-55 NKJV).

For those women who have been deceived that they are carrying a blob of tissue without identity in their wombs, notice that John in the womb recognized Jesus in the womb and leaped for joy.

God can use the hungry, the disadvantaged, the poor, the hopeless, the disabled, and the lowly for His purpose. God can use you and me. Anticipate your response, prepare to be used, and hope for His call.

UNHEALTHY DESIRE

Here is a warning about hope: hope can turn into an obsession, an unhealthy desire to have not what one needs, but extras or extravagances. Hope can become an unhealthy desire to have. This unhealthy desire creeps up to covetousness, which is forbidden by Ten Commandments. "You shall not covet your neighbor's house; you shall not covet your neighbor's wife, nor his male servant, nor his female servant, nor his ox, nor his donkey, nor anything that *is* your neighbor's" (Ex 20:17 NKJV).

> Matthew Henry says that the tenth commandment strikes at the root: thou shalt not covet. This commandment forbids all inordinate desire of having that which will be a gratification to ourselves. "Oh, that such a man's house were mine! Such a man's wife mine! Such a man's estate mine!" This is certainly the language of discontent with our own lot and envy of our neighbor's; and these are the sins principally forbidden here (by the tenth commandment).[1]

Coveting does not end with possessions, houses, estates, or money. It continues with intangible objects, like hoping for fame, praying for intelligence, or seeking power. Jesus dealt with the similar intangible desire of two of his disciples, who wanted to be great in the kingdom of God.

The mother of Zebedee's sons came to Jesus, asking Him to grant that her two sons might sit, one on His right hand and the other on His left, in His kingdom. Jesus told her that she did not know what she was asking. He questioned whether her the two sons would be able to endure the struggle ahead. Her sons responded that they were able. Jesus said that seats to His right and left were not His to give.

When the other ten disciples heard this discussion, they were greatly displeased with the brothers. Jesus said that the rulers of the Gentiles exercised power and authority over them, but the disciples were not to act in that way. Whoever desired to become great should become a servant, and whoever desired to be first should become a slave. As an example Jesus said that the Son of Man did not come to be served, but to serve others, and to give His life as a ransom for many (see Mt 20:20–28).

Whoever wishes to be great must become a servant. With a servant attitude, one's entire life changes. This change is wrought by the Holy Spirit, who moves the heart to compassion for the poor, the widow, and the fatherless. An employee with a servant attitude will always find work. Employers hate to lose a person who serves the customer, the company, and the other employees. In addition, a servant-minded person will produce higher-quality items in production and receive higher satisfaction from customers, because the person will do his or her best.

The home life of a Spirit-inspired person will also be of high quality. A servant-minded man will encourage his wife to speak, and he will listen. He will attempt to please her in the Lord. Thankfulness, loveliness, and praise to God will rule the lives of family members.

When we are servant-minded, our hope will be established in contentment, no matter what our personal circumstances. However, contentment does not come to us as we sit on the couch, watching television. It comes in service to others. Our hope comes to us through the Holy Spirit giving us strength to accept tribulation, to serve others, and to turn the hearts of our enemies into the hearts of friends. Our hope comes from being useful, kind, and loving in the community. It comes from trusting Jesus for our daily bread.

My daughter has lived with me since her divorce. It has been a great blessing to me, especially after my wife died of cancer. Her two children also live here part-time, in a shared custody arrangement. We live in a large two-story home with a full basement. Although my daughter says she loves the home and wants to keep it up after I die, the property is a lot of work. I needed to find a way to increase the income from my assets so that, after I die, she can keep the home.

The idea came to me to room-share. I have counseled others who are having financial issues to bring in a roommate to share living costs. So I invested in a downstairs kitchen, fake wood flooring, carpet, and a sink that drains upward, since we are on a septic system. I set up the bunkbeds we used years ago and furnished the rest of the space. Then I rented the space to a man and his child at a low weekly rent, with all utilities paid. This brought in additional income and hope for my daughter's future. It also gave me the ability to provide low-cost housing to a family in need, enabling the man to pay down his debts. He stayed for more than a year and moved out leaving the property vacant.

More than a year later, one of my daughter's friends was divorcing and needed a place to stay. The friend had three children and a dog, and had not worked for many years. She moved in to our basement space. It was a godsend for her. She lived there for free until she got a job. She has been a godsend to my daughter too, because she is able to talk to her and help her with the problems of the day.

A miracle starts by looking around the house and finding items that are available. There are more and more retired folks in homes that have space available for a second family. If you need to save on housing, then I suggest you consider room- or home-sharing.

CHAPTER NINE

GUILT, FORGIVENESS, AND RESTORATION

FINANCIAL GUILT

Financial guilt comes from being responsible for an offense or wrongdoing. It is the feeling of regret for having committed an improper act, a recognition of one's own financial responsibility for doing something wrong.

The underlying premise is that there is indeed a right way and a wrong way. For those of us who still need to learn right from wrong, we have governments that dictate and devise laws identifying what, in their judgment, is wrong. However, governmental laws are made by people, and those people have their selfish interests to accomplish.

There are also moral laws that have been written on the hearts and in the minds of people throughout the generations and throughout the civilizations, from the beginning of recorded time. Moral laws relate to the practice, manners, or conduct of people as social beings in relation to each other. There are right and wrong behaviors stemming from the Golden Rule: do unto others as you would have them do unto you.

God has given us moral laws to live by, involving all people. Here is Martin Luther's gloss on the Ten Commandments:

1. We should fear, love, and trust God above anything else.
2. We are to fear and love God so that we do not use His name superstitiously, or use it to curse, swear, lie, or deceive, but call on Him in prayer, praise, and thanksgiving.
3. We are to fear and love God so that we do not neglect His Word and the preaching of it, but regard His Word as holy and gladly hear it and learn it.
4. We are to fear and love God so that we do not despise and anger our parents and others in authority, but respect, obey, love, and serve them.
5. We are to fear and love God so that we do not hurt our neighbor in any way, but help him in all his physical needs.
6. We are to fear and love God so that in matters of sex, our words and conduct are pure and honorable, and husband and wife love and respect each other.
7. We are to fear and love God so that we do not take our neighbor's money or property or get them in any dishonest way, but help him to improve and protect his property and means of making a living.
8. We are to fear and love God so that we do not betray, slander, or lie about our neighbor, but defend him, speak well of him, and explain his actions in the kindest possible way.
9. We are to fear and love God so that we do not desire to get our neighbor's possessions by scheming, or by pretending to have a right to them, but always help him keep what is his.
10. We are to fear and love God so that we do not tempt or coax away from our neighbor his wife or his workers, but encourage them to remain loyal.[1]

We should follow these commandments and take personal responsibility to obey them. We should feel remorse, guilt, and anguish when we do not obey God, the source of these rules for living. Each commandment has financial implications.

Guilt and anguish separate us from God and create barriers from receiving a financial miracle and all God's good gifts. We are restored to fellowship with Jesus when we repent of our wrong actions and seek His forgiveness. The Ten Commandments cannot be obeyed without power from the Holy Spirit, who provides us with new hearts.

Find a church that offers forgiveness of sins during the worship service.

Ask yourself: Do your actions, discussions, interactions, work, prayers, language, tone, dress, leadership, interests, thoughts, transactions, savings, contributions, and attitudes glorify God?

I remember seeing a cartoon with a little angel standing on the right shoulder of a person and a little devil standing on the left shoulder. Each was whispering influence and ideas into the man's ears, attempting to lead him into light or into darkness. One voice urged productive work, the other tempted with schemes of something for nothing. Honor or dishonor? Love or hate? Selfishness or selflessness? Receiving or giving? Obedience or disobedience? Godliness or ungodliness?

It is very hard to resist temptation because we each have lusts for money and pleasure. Remember, these are natural inclinations of the heart. Today we are tempted over the internet with enticing graphics, fake endorsements of products, false pretenses about guarantees, and fake news telling only a portion of the true story. All temptations revolve around financial gain, for the love of money is the root of all evil (see 1 Tm 6:10).

If you give in to a financial scam, creating guilt, attempt to learn a lesson and to sharpen your guard against such evil, but do not fall into remorse and depression about the matter. Live and learn. God still provides.

Scams abound and include charitable and political organizations that claim to do good in the world. I use the company Charity Navigator to research not-for-profit organizations (NPOs). Charity Navigator gives me information about an NPO's tax forms, which are required to be public in many cases. Such forms include disclosures about executive compensation and what percentage of revenues go to the need in question.

YOU HAVE A CHOICE

Joshua became the leader of the nation of Israel after Moses, during the time the nation entered the Promised Land. God gave them the directive to thoroughly destroy all the nations that already inhabited the land. The reason for such complete destruction was to eliminate the influence of foreign gods and rituals. It is interesting that today we welcome foreign gods and rituals. Our nation is turning away from the true God with an objective to be inclusive and diversified. Other religions are held as legitimate and acceptable, and sinful behaviors escape comment and correction.

With a stern warning, Moses set before the Israelites a choice: life or death, blessing or curse. Moses said to choose life and live (see Dt 30:19).

It is impossible to choose life consistently and keep the Lord's commandants, because we are born with sin passed down from Adam and Eve. Sin takes the form of selfishness, self-centeredness, self-love, and greed, resulting in depravity. We are tempted continually to follow other ways of life—to gamble, to accumulate wealth, to focus on a retirement lifestyle, and to spend on entertainment. The church is subject to these temptations just as people are.

Without some form of outside intervention to change the makeup of our hearts, we are doomed to destruction and will bring down those around us.

God has provided a way out of our dilemma through Jesus

Christ, who died by painful crucifixion for our transgressions. Jesus took on the sins of the world and became our substitute as the target for God's wrath, which we deserve. The price for our sins has been paid, and we are set free from being slaves to sin. When we believe that Jesus is the Son of God, the Holy Spirit will dwell within us, giving us strength to fight the devil and his agents.

What choices do you make that help or hurt yourself and others? Do you choose life with God through faith in Jesus?

When I was with a consumer counseling firm, I counseled a lady who was deep in debt due to online gambling. After incurring a small debt, she tried harder to win back the loss. This effort resulted in more loss. The temptation to gamble was sitting in her house, luring her with fancy graphics, testimonies of winners, moving pictures, excitement, and grand enticement, to the point that it was impossible to resist. My advice was to get rid of the computer, the monitor, and everything related to the gambling activity. I urged her to throw it out and get a job with long hours to keep hands and mind occupied. If she needed to check email, she could go to the library.

Before 1964 no state had a lottery.[2] Times have changed. Gambling has probably brought many people to poverty while making governments rich. Do governments really care about their citizens? Does Washington DC really care about financial responsibility and good stewardship?

Another note about gambling is that the machines are set to take in more than they pay out. The house will always win in the long term. The percentage payout can be set and changed. I noticed that the manager of a small grocery store put in a Keno machine. I questioned him about the matter, saying that customers would play the gambling machine with their grocery money. He said, if I recall correctly, that the machine was set for a 35 percent payout or a 65 percent losing rate. If a person plays thirty-five times, will the person be guaranteed a win? Does a second play increase the chances winning? No. The number of times one plays does not affect the chances of winning. The winning percentage stays the same for each play. The excitement of winning is addictive.

For many of us, we need to destroy the temptation, run away, change the subject, or bring another person into the room to distract us. I have a sweet tooth and love desserts. After a family gathering, we had four partial pies, cookies, and a pumpkin roll filled with sweet icing in our kitchen. Now, the grandchildren go to school and my daughter goes to work, leaving me alone most of the day with those sweets on the counter. After several days, I threw out all those delicious temptations in order to stop gaining weight.

I suggest we make a bedrock decision. This is a decision we research and dig deeper to understand until we reach a firm foundation. A bedrock decision is made only once. It stands on a firm foundation for the rest of one's life. An example of a bedrock decision is not to smoke and not to take drugs. Years ago, I made a bedrock decision not to gamble or play the lottery.

DEALING WITH GUILT

The only way to deal with financial guilt is to understand the forgiveness of sins, including financial sins. Forgiveness begins with repentance or a sorrowful response to our sinful actions. We seek forgiveness and pledge to turn in a new direction, to do the next right thing.

Being an older man, I can look back on my life and question my actions that resulted in financial guilt. Why did I not see the sickness of some of the animals we owned, resulting in their misery? Could I not have taken financial action by changing their situation in our home or seeking professional help? I have guilt.

Why did I fuss about the cost of buying my son a "Starter" jacket when he was in middle school? He was short in stature, and the jacket provided some self-confidence and status. I should have eagerly purchased anything he needed. I have guilt.

Why did I accept the church bookkeeping position as a volunteer, consuming me with such a workload that I missed much of my child's early years? I have guilt.

After my wife died of cancer, I realized we had missed out on friendship, joy, and laughter. We should have both set aside our workloads and dated, spending money on ourselves with dinners, shows, and trips. I have guilt.

I was shopping at a Kroger, and a young lady came up to me. She showed me a note that said she spoke only French, and her husband and young baby were in the car and needed food. We went throughout the store, buying baby diapers, roasted chicken (which they could eat in the car that night), peanut butter and bread (I insisted), Oreos (which I approved), and other items. We went to the car, which was a station wagon with the back made into a bed. I put the groceries on the bed and talked about where they were going to sleep that night. I cannot remember the answer. He spoke English, and I asked to see the baby. The baby was a tiny newborn, sleeping in a box or something other than a car seat. How far they were going and where, I cannot remember. I do remember the baby in the box.

Oh, why did I not take them into my house? We had plenty of room. We could have financially cared for them and attempted to understand their situation. Were they running from something or running to somewhere? Oh, why did I not help more, including providing money? I have guilt.

Sin lies in not doing something good as well as in doing something bad. Sin also includes improper thoughts.

To dwell on past sins, past opportunities lost, past mistakes, and past reckless behavior will result in depression, unproductivity, mental anguish, and a separation from God, thwarting financial miracles and faith.

The Christian has a compassionate, loving God who is eager to forgive sin. This is permanent forgiveness from the One who matters—God. It will restore you to faith and righteousness.

ADULTERY AND MURDER

Is it possible for God to forgive someone who commits adultery? How about murder? In the Bible, there is an account of King David committing adultery with Bathsheba. In the cover-up, David commits the murder of Uriah, Bathsheba's husband.

First we must review some of David's life experiences and his relationship with God. King Saul was the first appointed king of Israel, with kingly stature and appearance. Here is a paragraph from the *Life Application Bible*: "During his reign he had his greatest successes when he obeyed God. His greatest failures resulted from acting on his own. Saul had the raw materials to be a good leader—appearance, courage, and action. Even his weaknesses could have been used by God if Saul had recognized them and left them in God's hands. His own choices cut him off from God and eventually alienated him from his own people."[3]

While Saul was still king of Israel, David—as a youth, a shepherd, the eighth child of Jesse—was anointed by the prophet Samuel to be king over Israel. Samuel took a horn of oil and anointed David in the midst of his brothers. This was humiliating to the older brothers, since David was the least of his family and unimpressive. From the day of anointing onward, the Holy Spirit came upon David (see 1 Sm 16:13). If you are weak and unimpressive, be encouraged, because God's strength is achieved in weakness. We will know for certain when our personal project has been under God's watch when suddenly we see significant results.

Notice that God rejected Saul, who was previously anointed by God, because of disobedience. Notice that the Spirit of the Lord came upon David from the day of his anointing through the rest of his life, despite adultery and murder and other mistakes he made.

The *Life Application Bible* notes:

> What made God refer to David as a man after my own heart (Acts 13:22)? David, more than

anything else, had an unchangeable belief in the faithful and forgiving nature of God. He was a man who lived with great zest. He sinned many times, but was quick to confess his sins. His confessions were from the heart, and his repentance was genuine. David never took God's forgiveness lightly or his blessing for granted. In return, God never held back either his forgiveness or the consequences of his actions. David experienced the joy of forgiveness even when he had to suffer the consequences of his sins.[4]

Some of the consequences David suffered for the sins of adultery and murder included the death of his child with Bathsheba, and the Lord raising up adversity against him from within his own house (see 2 Sm 12:10–15).

David wrote Psalm 51 after this adultery and murder. He wrote in repentance and sought forgiveness. The psalm asks for mercy and uses a basic value to support his case: he asks God to judge him according to God's lovingkindness and tender mercies, which David is confident will blot out his sins. David admits his sins and indicates sin is always against God (see Ps 51:1–4).

Continuing with Psalm 51, King David writes the following humble and pleading words:

> Create in me a clean heart, O God, And renew a steadfast spirit within me. Do not cast me away from Your presence, And do not take Your Holy Spirit from me. Restore to me the joy of Your salvation, And uphold me *by Your* generous Spirit (Ps 51:10–12 NKJV).

It seems to me there are no more meaningful words of repentance than these. In our church service, these words are often sung as part of the liturgy. Remember that from the lineage of David came our Savior, Jesus Christ. The point of this narrative is that we sin. We have guilt. Sinful actions separate us from God and His benefits, blessings, and abundant life. When we repent, recognizing our financial sins, responsibilities, and choices, we can be restored by seeking forgiveness.

To avoid guilt, always do your very best in every situation, trusting Jesus with the outcome of your efforts, which may not appear for years to come. Remember Abraham, who received God's promise to have descendants as numerous as the stars. He died after fathering two children. One was with Hagar, the slave woman. The other was by the promise, since Abraham and Sarah were both too old to have children, but God delivered anyway. The answer to prayer that you have been waiting for may not come until after you are dead.

CHAPTER TEN

NEARER TO GOD THROUGH PRAYER

GETTING CLOSE TO GOD

Oh, how I wish I could get close to a God who is merciful, gracious, and slow to anger. He does not deal with me according to my many sins. He is a forgiving Father who has unending love for me. He provides amazing grace: listening to my deepest emotions, helping in time of need, responding with answers to prayer, anticipating my next project, sustaining me with daily bread, showing me financial miracles, leading me with my gut, putting opportunities for service in my path, and testing me according to obedience. He calms the rough seas, since my Father is in the boat with me. He gives me power to keep my mouth shut, to be thankful for losses, and to love my neighbor, even in difficult situations. Oh, how I wish I could get close to the triune God: God the Father, God Jesus Christ, and God the Holy Spirit.

As the heavens are far above the earth, to the moon and beyond, so great is His mercy toward me if I am connected to Him with fear, respect, devotion, and dependence. God is on my mind all day long. I thank Him for finding my missing pieces and helping with my tasks of the day. He puts little things in order, giving me the right words to say to a child with a broken heart, mercy for a child that has had another spill, and strength for the next home task. I witness His financial miracles daily. Little things appear to make the task at hand profitable. He provides me a good night's rest. Oh, how I want to be close to the God of the Psalms.

It might seem difficult or even impossible, with our depraved human nature, to get close to God using our own effort. And guess what? It *is* impossible. God reaches out to us first and draws us to Himself, using the Holy Spirit. He puts people in our path to help lead the way.

Without you asking, someone answers a religious question you have been thinking about. You accidentally turn on a religious song that touches your heart. You flip through the television channels and find interest in a preacher. A coworker in the lunchroom makes a remark that pulls you toward God. God finds you in these and many other ways. God wants you to be interested in the grace He has available for you.

These interactions, along with the Word of God and preaching, demonstrate the Holy Spirit at work. The work of the Holy Spirit continues throughout one's life in a process called *sanctification*, which is a long religious term for a process that makes one more Christ-like. Sanctification prepares each of us for service to our neighbors, with a future look to heaven.

Martin Luther, in *The Large Catechism*, discusses our helpless estate without the Holy Spirit:

> For neither you nor I could ever know anything of Christ, or believe on Him, and obtain Him for our Lord, unless it were offered to us and granted to our hearts by the Holy Ghost through the preaching of the Gospel. The work is done and accomplished; for Christ has acquired and gained the treasure for us by His suffering, death, resurrection, etc. But if the work remained concealed so that no one

knew of it, then it would be in vain and lost. That this treasure, therefore, might not lie buried, but be appropriated and enjoyed, God has caused the Word to go forth and be proclaimed, in which He gives the Holy Ghost to bring this treasure home and appropriate it to us. Therefore sanctifying is nothing else than bringing us to Christ to receive this good, to which we could not attain of ourselves.[1]

At some point in your life, there will occur an event that puts you in a seat in front of the preacher. This could be a funeral, a wedding, a follow-up on an invitation from someone in the church, a public entertainment, a vacation Bible school, a crusade, or merely curiosity about the local church.

AN EVENT

In my case, the event was the birth of our son. In my youth, I attended church with my parents and learned about baptism as being something important. After the baptism of our son, my wife and I started attending church. The unexpected took place. A concept took me off guard. It was something I did not understand and never expected: I realized my corrupt and sinful nature.

Oh my. I was suddenly faced with a terrified consciousness of my sinful nature compared to a holy, holy, holy God. Woe was me! My reaction was similar to the reaction of Isaiah, described in Isaiah 6:3, when he had a vision of the Lord in the Temple, the train of His robe filling the space. The seraphim called to one to another, "Holy, holy, holy is the Lord!" The voice of him who cried out shook the posts of the Temple, and smoke filled the room. Isaiah said, "Woe *is* me, for I am undone! Because I *am* a man of unclean lips, and I dwell in the midst of a people of unclean lips" (Is 6:5 NKJV).

Isaiah came face to face with the Lord, and the contrast between earthly creatures and a holy God is fearful.

Why was this so startling to me? It was startling because my wife and I were living a decent life. There were no drugs, no drunkenness, no foul language, and no fighting. We worked hard at our jobs, paid our rent on time, took care of the cars, watched our spending, paid our taxes, smiled, said good morning, followed the rules at work, went home for the holidays—need I go on?

Where was God in our lives? The simple answer was nowhere. There was no prayer, no means of grace, no Holy Communion, no preaching, no reading of the Bible, no spiritual music, no worship, and no religious television. We did not feel the need for God. Everything was just fine. We were doing well, all the bills were paid, and we were satisfied.

Did we ask for a financial miracle? I am sure we did, because at the time the firm I was working for did not pay me enough to cover our bills. It was the only time I ever asked for a raise. The other firms I worked for over the years provided me with increases based on my production and efforts, without me asking.

Where was guilt? We did not have any, since we had done nothing deserving a guilty judgment. The civil laws were honored. But how about spiritual laws?

God provided the Ten Commandments to his chosen people, the Israelites, after freeing them from four hundred years of slavery. He brought them out of bondage with a powerful hand, using the plagues and wonders against the slave masters. God guided the Israelites safely across the Red Sea. God led them with a cloud during the day and fire by night.

The commandments tell us not to kill. Have I killed anyone? No. But Jesus expands the commandment to include getting angry at anyone. Of that, I am guilty.

The commandments tell us not to commit adultery. Have I committed adultery? No. But Jesus includes improper looking at a pretty women as a form of adultery. Of that, I am guilty.

The commandments tell us to keep holy the Sabbath day. Have I remembered the Sabbath day and kept it holy? Of that, I am guilty.

I am guilty of breaking every commandment. The commandments were not made to justify us in front of God by keeping them, but to condemn us. As it says in the Bible, there is no one righteous; no, not even one (see Rom 3:10–12). We have all gone astray.

In order for us to get close to God, God had to take the first action. Jesus the Son came to earth in humility as a baby and received the wrath of God the Father, who substituted Jesus for us. Jesus took on the sins of the world, now and in the future. The wrath of God was laid on Jesus for our sinfulness.

For our part, we must follow the leading of the Holy Spirit, repent of our sins and live lives of faithfulness, including prayer, worship, receipt of the sacraments, and reading of the Bible. At some point the Holy Spirit will indwell us, giving us a "New Financial Nature", in which answers to prayer are expected by faith. Income, spending, saving, and giving are marvelously accomplished, with balance, and in favor with God. We are saved by grace through faith, and faith is not from our own effort, but a gift from God.

After regeneration by the Holy Spirit, we begin a life of prayer. We think of God and thank Him all day long.

PRAYER

Matthew George Easton, in his *Easton's Illustrated Dictionary of the Bible*, defines *prayer* as a conversation with God; the intercourse of the soul with God, not in contemplation or meditation, but in direct address to him. Prayer may be oral or mental, occasional or constant, ejaculatory or formal. It is a "beseeching the Lord" (Ex 32:11);

"pouring out the soul before the Lord" (1 Sm 1:15); "praying and crying to heaven" (2 Chr 32:20); "seeking unto God and making supplication" (Job 8:5); "drawing near to God" (Ps 73:28); "bowing the knees" (Eph 3:14).

Prayer presupposes a belief in the personality of God, his ability and willingness to hold intercourse with us, his personal control of all things and of all his creatures and all their actions.

Acceptable prayer must be sincere (Heb 10:22), offered with reverence and godly fear, with a humble sense of our own insignificance as creatures and of our own unworthiness as sinners, with earnest importunity, and with unhesitating submission to the divine will. Prayer must also be offered in the faith that God is, and is the hearer and answerer of prayer, and that he will fulfil his word, "Ask, and ye shall receive" (Mat 7:7, 8; Mat 21:22; Mark 11:24; John 14:13, 14), and in the name of Christ (John 16:23, 24; John 15:16; Eph 2:18; Eph 5:20; Col 3:17; 1 Pt 2:5).[2]

Prayer provides power in the lives of Christians. This power results in financial miracles—not miracles like winning the lottery, but power to defeat the temptation to play the lottery. Not power to have or covet to have property like the rich and famous, but power to become happy and satisfied with the property we have.

An employer will consider it a financial miracle if an employee wants to work, shows up awake, dresses appropriately, arrives on time, learns the trade, commits himself to the task, avoids abuse of the telephone, refuses to steal, refrains from complaining, accepts correction, and demonstrates a willing attitude to serve customers and staff. The power of God can regenerate you into an ideal employee with a bright future.

"God has spoken once, Twice I have heard this: That power belongs to God" (Ps 62:11 NKJV). The power of God through prayer is discussed in the book *How to Obtain Fullness of Power*, by R. A. Torrey. Torrey agrees that power belongs to God, based on the psalm above. However, he says that this power can become part of our lives if we ask. God holds out His full hands and says, "It will be given to you if you ask. You will find it if you seek. It will be opened for you if you knock" (see Mt 7:7). Jesus also makes a comparison between a lower man and a higher God. If lower man, who is evil, can do good things, then your Father, who is holy and in heaven, will give even greater good gifts to those who ask (see Mt 7:11).

The poverty and powerlessness of the average Christian finds its explanation in the words of the apostle James, who says that we lust and do not have, we covet and cannot obtain, and we fight and do not have because we do not ask (see Jas 4:2).

R. A. Torrey identifies several directions for the power of prayer available for us:

1. Prayer has power to bring true knowledge of ourselves and our needs. There is nothing more necessary than that we know ourselves, our weakness, our sinfulness, and our selfishness. We must know that in us—that is to say, in our flesh—dwells no good thing (see Rom 7:18).
2. Prayer has power to cleanse our hearts from sin, both secret sin and known sin (see Ps 19:12–13).
3. Prayer has power to hold us up in our goings, and give us victory over temptation (see Ps 17:5).
4. Prayer has power to govern our tongues. Many Christians who have desired fullness of power in Christian life and service have found themselves kept from it by unruly tongues.

5. Prayer has power to bring us wisdom. The Word of God is very explicit on this point. In the letter to James, it says that if any lack wisdom, let them ask of God (see Jas 1:5).
6. Prayer has power to open our eyes to behold wondrous things out of God's Word (see Ps 119:18).
7. Prayer has power to bring the Holy Spirit, in all His blessed power and manifold gracious operations, into our hearts and lives (see Lk 11:13).
8. Prayer has power to bring the fullness of God's power into our work.
9. Prayer has power to bring salvation to others.[3]

George Müller, whom I discussed in a previous chapter, created the "five conditions of prevailing prayer," which are helpful in understanding prayer that works. The five conditions are:

1. Entire dependence upon the merits and mediation of the Lord Jesus Christ as the only ground of any claim for blessing (see Jn 14:13, 14, 15:16, etc.).
2. Separation from all known sin—if we regard iniquity in our hearts, the Lord will not hear us, for it would be sanctioning sin (see Ps 66:18).
3. Faith in God's word of promise as confirmed by His oath—not to believe Him is to make Him both a liar and a perjurer (see Heb 11:6, 6:13–20).
4. Asking in accordance with His will—our motives must be godly, and we must not seek any gift of God to consume it upon our lusts (see 1 Jn 5:14; Jas 4:3).
5. Importunity in supplication—waiting on God and waiting for God, as the husbandman has long patience to wait for the harvest (see Jas 5:7; Lk 18:1–8).[4]

MODEL PRAYER

Prayer is one way to get close to God, but how do we start to pray? What is effective prayer? Does God hear us? How do we organize a prayer? When are prayers answered? What hinders prayer? To help us with these questions, I have researched several model prayers and articles about developing a life of prayer and closeness to God. Financial miracles come from God. We must get close to God to know His will for us, to know His ever-presence with us, and to receive His power to accomplish His will.

Billy Graham answered a question about prayer using his website: please tell me how I can learn to pray properly. I try to pray, but after about a minute or so, I run out of things to say. I know God must be very disappointed in me.

Answer: When you were very young, did you suddenly start talking with your parents in long sentences? I doubt it. And yet they weren't disappointed in you; they were delighted in your first attempts to speak.

In the same way, when we truly understand that God is our loving, heavenly Father and we are His children, then we won't worry so much about running out of things to say or disappointing Him. God takes delight in us when we come to Him in prayer. When His disciples asked Jesus how to pray, He replied, "This, then, is how you should pray: 'Our Father in heaven...'" (Mt 6:9).

1. Begin when you pray by thanking and praising God for His love and goodness. The psalmist wrote, "Oh that men would give thanks to the LORD for his goodness, and for His wonderful works to the children of men!" (Ps 107:8 NKJV).
2. Then confess your sins and ask for His forgiveness.
3. Finally, bring your concerns to Him including the concerns for others.

Perhaps, however, the first prayer you need to make is one of faith, asking Christ to come into your life and giving yourself to Him. Christ has opened heaven's door for us by His death on the cross. When we know Him, we know God hears our prayers.[5]

I attempt to get close to God through prayer. I enjoy my time in prayer in the morning. I sit on the porch with my loyal dog, who weighs about eleven pounds, sleeping on my lap.

ACTS

Another model prayer is **ACTS**, an acronym standing for *a*doration with *c*onfession, *t*hanksgiving, and *s*upplication. I found the information on the Got Questions website and summarize below.

1. *Adoration* means "worship"—glorifying and exalting God. Through adoration, we show our loyalty and admiration of our Father. As we pray, we are called to worship God in adoration. This could be a declaring His attributes or other forms of worship.

2. *Confession* means "to agree with." When we confess our sins, we agree with God that we are wrong and that we have sinned against Him by what we have said, thought, or done. With our repentance, God forgives us and restores our fellowship with Him.

3. *Thanksgiving* also means "worship." How is thanksgiving different from adoration? The difference is that adoration focuses on who God is; thanksgiving focuses on what God has done.

4. *Supplication* refers to prayer for the needs of ourselves and others. A supplication is a request or petition.
   a. We may pray for leading (see Ps 5:8).
   b. We may pray for wisdom (see Jas 1:5).

c. We may, as Paul encouraged us to do, make "supplication for all the saints," meaning to pray diligently for our brothers and sisters in Christ (see Eph 6:18).

d. We may pray for mercy (see Ps 4:1).[6]

All prayers should be presented to God in the name of Jesus, who is our mediator. The only way to God is through the Son (see 1 Tm 2:5).

Getting close to God takes some initiative. The result is knowing the love of God, His desire to help, and His desire for us to depend on Him, including receiving the "New Financial Nature".

CHAPTER ELEVEN

NEARER TO GOD THROUGH GIVING

REGULAR AND PROPORTIONAL (RAP) GIVING

We need to get close to God so our prayers, supplications, petitions, and requests for financial miracles are in accordance with the will of God and are heard and considered. In the previous chapters, I discussed the means of grace, including baptism, the Lord's Supper, preaching, reading the Bible, and putting ourselves in front of the Word of God through television ministries, Christian music, Christian radio, family devotions, Sunday school, and participation with the local church through its outreach ministries.

There is another way to get close to God, which I call RAP giving. This is *regular and proportional* giving to the church and other Christian causes. It is based on the study of behavior in the real world, answering the question: Does your heart follow your money, or does your money follow your heart?

Let us look at some examples. You live in community with many houses and nice neighbors. One of the neighbors buys a pop-up tent camper. You notice the fun they are having and hear stories of camping life from the kids, including hiking, swimming, bicycling, sitting around campfires, visiting natural sites with breathtaking scenery, and other fun opportunities.

Soon you buy a camper also and enjoy the same activities. This takes time away from other activities and diverts your financial matters. Family resources go into camping. Soon the whole family loves camping. The heart follows your money. The same premise applies to all the world's pleasures.

Another example is professional sports. I used to be a fan of the Cleveland Browns football team when the team was the winningest in football history. The great Jimmy Brown wore number 32. I still have a program from the 1964 World Championship game of the National Football League, played on December 27, 1964, against the Baltimore Colts. Football fans spend money on game tickets, stadium meals, and transportation. More importantly, games require time, averaging several hours each. Often fans spend their entire Sunday afternoon in front of the television set.

As time went on, I found myself lunging at the television to recover a fumble. I would be so disappointed over a pass interception that I was grumpy after the game. Money and time commitment went first, and then the heart followed.

If we start regular and proportionate contributions to the church and other Christian causes, our hearts will follow, getting closer to God and closer to Christian services in the community.

We should give to the church and Christian causes first from our paychecks. Our paychecks are gifts from God, and we wish to thank God for His mercy in providing us with gainful employment. Therefore, when we get paid, we should set aside an amount immediately. Some families write a check immediately to put into the offering plate at the next church service. If one gets paid only once a month, then write four checks, one for each weekly service.

The idea of writing a check first is to tie together our paychecks with God's provision for us. It is difficult to see God in our lives, directly benefitting us. If one goes into the office and spends all day processing accounts information, it is difficult to see the connection between computer work and God's provision. A farmer can plant the seed, but it is a miracle of God that makes it grow. There is a direct connection between farm work and harvest. Not so with computer input. To connect our efforts to God's provision, we should make a financial contribution our first choice. This choice should be consistent and repeated.

As far as the proportion is concerned, it is up to the giver to establish the percentage of income to give. The percentage should be a decision made without compulsion, without duress, and without ungodly influence. Once the percentage is established, do not change it for the short term. Even if wages and commissions increase or decrease, keep the percentage consistent. The forced tithe is an Old Testament requirement. In the New Testament, we are under grace and love instead of law.

The heart of the giver will be pulled into the church because where your treasure is, there will be your heart.

RAP giving draws you and your family close to God. One passage of scripture says to draw near to God and He will draw close to you (see Jas 4:8). It emphasizes that the first decision is for us to take an action toward God. Another scripture passage says that where your treasure is, there your heart will be also (see Lk 12:34). It suggests we look at our checkbooks to see what we treasure.

When we employ RAP giving, we give up authority and redirect our money. We soon loosen the grip money has over our hearts and feel a sense of relief, realizing that all we have comes from God anyway. God provides our income. We also start to really see God's actions and financial miracles in our lives, because we draw closer to God.

I am a witness that God can provide for us through cancer treatments, significant business losses, bone marrow transplants, self-employment, and the day-to-day problems of scheduling family activities.

WISDOM

Solomon, King David's son, received blessings from God, including wisdom. The following narrative is adapted from 2 Chronicles 1:7–12.

After King David died, Solomon became king. God was with him and exalted him. Solomon spoke to all Israel. He went to the high place, to the tabernacle of the meeting place, to the altar before the Lord, and offered a thousand burnt offerings on it. "On that night God appeared to Solomon, and said to him, 'Ask! What shall I give you?'" (2 Chr 1:7 NKJV).

Solomon responded that God had shown mercy to his father, David, and had allowed Solomon to become king. But Solomon was overwhelmed by the task before him. He felt he did not have the knowledge to lead the people. So he asked for wisdom necessary to become worthy of God and to lead the people.

God answered that because Solomon's heart was interested in others and he had not asked for riches, long life, or victory over his enemies, God would grant his request and give him wisdom. God also gave Solomon riches and honor such as no other king had had before or would have after.

Wow! Solomon did not ask for a financial miracle, but God gave him one anyway. Perhaps we should not ask for financial miracles but for skills, energy, compassion, wisdom, and education. These gifts will enable us to do our tasks, jobs, and duties to the best of our abilities, and as a result, maybe God will grant us financial miracles also.

Amazingly, God started the conversation with a command: "Ask!" Can you imagine God coming to you by way of a meditation, a church service, or sermon with a very bold shout? I think God is asking each of us to tell Him our needs in specific requests that are according to God's will.

There is a psalm in which God calls to the nation of Israel to only listen to Him (see Ps 81). God requires that there shall be no foreign god among them, and they shall not worship a foreign god. God justifies the demand by saying He is the Lord their God, who brought them out of Egypt with wonders and amazement. He reminds them that He can help them with His strong arm. Then God proclaims that if they open their mouths, He will fill them (see Ps 81:8–10).

It seems to me God wants to help us and provide for everything we need if we ask and obey. However, do not ask for money or the financial death of your competitors. I ask God for help to understand my mission in life, help to direct my paths, help to fill me with enthusiasm for the task, help to reach out to the world with my message of the "New Financial Nature", and help to speak of financial love, financial obedience, and financial grace.

TRUE SATISFACTION

With the wisdom of Solomon, what can we learn about worldly activities, common tasks, pleasures of the world, and all important tasks of man? The book of the Bible in which Solomon answers these probing questions about life is Ecclesiastes.

> The words of the Preacher, the son of David, king in Jerusalem.
> "Vanity of vanities," says the Preacher; "Vanity of vanities, all *is* vanity."
> What profit has a man from all his labor In which he toils under the sun? (Eccl 1:1–3 NKJV).

The *Life Application Bible* provides a blueprint for the book of Ecclesiastes, showing that certain paths in life lead to emptiness. This profound book also helps us discover the true purpose in life. Such wisdom can spare us from the emptiness that results from a life without God. Solomon teaches that people will not find meaning in knowledge, money, pleasure, work, or popularity.

True satisfaction comes from knowing that what we are doing is part of God's purpose for our lives. This is a book that can free us from our scramble for power, approval, and money, and draw us closer to God.[1]

Donald R. Glenn writes that the Teacher in Ecclesiastes declared that everything is "meaningless" (NIV) or "vanity" (KJV, RSV, NASB, NKJV). This includes toil (1:14; 2:11, 17; 4:4, 7–8), wisdom (2:15), righteousness (8:14), wealth (2:26, 5:10, 6:2), prestige (4:16), pleasure (2:1–2), youth and vigor (11:10), life (6:12, 7:15, 9:9), and even the future after death (11:8).[2]

Here is Solomon's conclusion of the matter: "Let us hear the conclusion of the whole matter: Fear God and keep His commandments, For this is man's all. For God will bring every work into judgment, including every secret thing, whether good or evil" (Eccl 12:13-14 NKJV).

The enjoyment and satisfaction of life come as a gift of God to those who fear God and keep His commandments, summarized as loving your neighbor as yourself. Whatever we do, we should do for the glory of God. We should live our lives in the Holy Spirit. We receive the power of the Holy Spirit by getting close to God.

GET CLOSE TO GOD

There is an urgent and desperate need to get close to God. We avoid the meaninglessness and emptiness of life by receiving new life. We are born again with new hearts. Our new hearts reinterpret our situation, so we see our lives differently. Suddenly we receive satisfaction and fulfillment from the work of our hands. We find new meaning in life's activities. We accept our situations patiently, without bitterness. We begin to accomplish God's will for our lives, renewing loving relationships, caring for one another in families, and sharing the burdens of daily life. We are assured that God loves us. Jesus died for our sins, providing a place for us in God's mansion of many rooms through faith and not works.

If we desire to see and experience power in our lives, we must get close to God. We must eventually become totally dependent on Him, as the nation of Israel was in the desert. The Israelites escaped from Egypt and headed to the Promised Land, having been freed from slavery by God's mighty arm and fed daily by manna.

When you are selecting a church, I suggest finding a church with the Word of God, the Bible, as its basis for teaching and preaching. Find one that includes forgiveness of sins after confession and repentance. Find one that believes in the sacraments of baptism and the Lord's Supper as Jesus instituted. Find one with the Lord's Prayer included in the service with the prayers of the church. Find one where the congregation recites the statement of faith using the Apostles' Creed. Find one with opportunities for serving others. Develop a personal relationship with Jesus, our mediator with God. The only door to heaven is through Jesus.

Scripture discusses a relationship of trust and dependence on God. If one knows the name of Jesus, not just intellectually but with loyalty, obedience, and awe, then one will put trust in Him who does not forsake those who seek Him (see Ps 9:10). God is a shield to all who have faith and trust Him (see Ps 18:30). His shield protects us from the darts of the devil, such as bullying, snide remarks, criticism, and put-downs. Such remarks do not penetrate the mind and soul of the practicing Christian because we are assured of God's love and favor.

Because we trust in Him, the Lord delivers us (see Ps 37:40). The Lord is a stronghold in the day of trouble. A stronghold is a fortified place with thick walls and sentry posts to protect us—not from all financial loss, but from mental and spiritual harm. We can be positive, finding a remnant of good out of every loss. The Lord knows those who trust Him and can enter the stronghold (see Na 1:7).

CHAPTER TWELVE

FINANCIAL WORRY, PLANNING, AND TRUST

FINANCIAL WORRY

I suppose financial worry is the most prominent trigger for starting the quest for a financial miracle. The situation could be something that has happened in the past, and the worry is that the situation will return. The situation could be a present problem, and the worry is about handling the situation with limited resources. The situation could be something in the future that will require resources, and the worry is how to handle the future cost. There are past, present, and future worries.

In a remarkable passage of scripture, Jesus directly addressed worry. Leading up to it, Jesus says that no one can serve two masters. You cannot serve God with wholehearted devotion, accomplishing His mission for you, and at the same time have a mind focused on wealth creation, dreaming about retirement and money-getting. If one is focused on money-getting, then one is probably worried because there is never enough coming in and there are financial setbacks continually.

The following is adapted from Matthew 6:25–32. Jesus first tells us not to worry about our lives, what we eat, or what we drink. Jesus then tells us not to worry about our bodies and what clothes we put on. Life is more than food, and the body is more than clothing. It is possible to interpret these sentences as stern commands from God.

Jesus uses an example of the birds. Birds do not reap or gather into barns, yet the heavenly Father feeds them. Are you not more valuable than they? Jesus asks who can add one foot to his height by worrying. His point is that worrying is futile and can accomplish nothing.

Jesus uses a second example about the lilies of the field. They neither work nor spin, yet they are more beautiful than the glory of Solomon. If God clothes the grass of the field, which dries up and is thrown into the oven for a fast burn, then will He not clothe you of little faith?

The Gentiles, Jesus says, seek these things. Your heavenly Father knows you need them. "But seek first the kingdom of God and His righteousness, and all these things shall be added to you" (Mt 6:33 NKJV).

The *Bible Knowledge Commentary* helps explain this amazing passage about worry:

> If a person is occupied with the things of God, the true Master, how will he care for his ordinary needs in life, such as food, clothing, and shelter? The Pharisees in their pursuit of material things had never learned to live by faith. Jesus told them and us not to worry about these things, for life is more important than physical things. He cited several illustrations to prove His point. The birds of the air are fed by the heavenly Father, and the lilies of the field grow in such a way that their splendor is greater than even Solomon's. Jesus was saying God has built into His Creation the means by which all things are cared for. The birds

are fed because they diligently work to maintain their lives. They do not store up great amounts of food, but continually work. And believers are far more valuable to God than birds! The lilies grow daily through a natural process. Therefore an individual need not be anxious about his existence (Mt 6:31), for by worrying he can never add any amount of time, not even a single hour, to his life. Rather than being like the pagans who are concerned about physical needs, the Lord's disciples should be concerned about the things of God, His kingdom and His righteousness. Then all these needs will be supplied in God's timing. This is the life of daily faith.[1]

DO YOUR VERY BEST

A long time ago, when I was first starting out in public accounting, I was somewhat dissatisfied with the work load and not excited about the myriad professional rules of engagement. I was, perhaps, spinning in a sea of uncertainty, self-examination, and exhaustion.

Then I had a revelation. For some reason, I was an hour late in the morning, driving to an audit of a local college. I was on the interstate heading around Columbus when I thought of the scripture passage above and exclaimed, "God, make me a bird and feed me!" I thought that being a bird at the dinner table of my heavenly Father would be a good resolution to my dilemma.

I then thought of how God fed birds. I realized that God did not exactly feed them. He made food available, but gathering it required the birds to work, and work very hard—in rain, heat, cold, wind, snow, drought, and all sort of circumstances. Without self-pity, without realizing they were having a tough time, birds found the food and ate it. God required the birds to do their best with the skills and instincts endowed upon them. If they did their best, they would eat.

On that day, I created a slogan for life: "Do your very best, and the very best will do unto you."

I began serving a new boss that day: God. If I served Him in my work, pleased Him, glorified Him, and gave Him credit for any success, then He would feed me, providing daily bread, which means all the things necessary for life.

My circumstances changed. When you do your best every day, the boss, peers, customers, suppliers, and family take notice. Energy increases, the mind is sharper, gossip is eliminated, focus increases, complaints subside, cooperation increases, worries disappear, and opportunities appear, including financial miracles. When you do your best at home, the kids become interesting instead of aggravating. Personal time spent on sports decreases. One-on-one time with the kids increases. Marriage commitment grows. Work around the house becomes a service to the family. Money discussions subside. Learning becomes important. Giving to the church becomes a priority. Fellowship with the church family is important. In general, a new heart is formed, and we become born-again with a "New Financial Nature".

In reflection, by doing your best and making God your boss, you accomplish the essence of seeking first the kingdom of God and His righteousness.

KNOWLEDGE OF THE FATHER

Albert Barnes comments that those who are destitute of the true doctrines of religion, unacquainted with proper dependence on Divine Providence, make it their chief concern to seek food and clothing. But those who have knowledge of our Father in heaven, who know that He will provide for our wants, should not be anxious. God has control over all things, and He can give you that which you need. He will give you that which He deems best for you.[2]

William Barclay comments that Jesus advances a very fundamental argument against worry. Worry, he says, is characteristic of a heathen, and not of one who knows what God is like. Worry is essentially distrust of God. Such distrust may be understandable in a heathen, who believes in a jealous, capricious, unpredictable god; but it is beyond comprehension in one who has learned to call God by the name of Father. The Christian cannot worry, because he believes in the love of God. We have seen how a great love can drive out every other concern. Such a love can inspire a man's work, intensify his study, purify his life, and dominate his whole being. It was Jesus's conviction that worry is banished when God becomes the dominating power of our lives.[3]

WORRY AND PLANNING

There is a difference between worrying about financial affairs and planning solutions. I am a former Certified Financial Planner™ and understand that there are steps to take in organizing financial affairs, including:

1. setting financial goals, such as living within your means, saving for purchases, and planning for retirement
2. gathering data, including balances in accounts, employer plans, and insurance products
3. performing financial calculations with assumptions about variables such as interest rates, tax rates, saving amounts, growth in spending and investment yields
4. making recommendations with regard to bank accounts, trust accounts, budgets, employer benefits, wills, medical plans, insurance plans, and investment alternatives
5. implementing choices through bank officers, attorneys, and documents
6. updating to reflect changing goals, impossible combinations, and new assumptions.

Preparation and planning slow down the worrying process because we become prepared and understand our limitations. However, without God, our plans will fail, since we are using human resources and human energy rather than trust in God. A sudden tragedy or a turn in events can stop the financial planning process. With change, we start over.

At one time I had a planning book with goals in separate areas, such as work goals, family goals, church goals, and education goals. Within each area, I listed specific steps to take to accomplish each goal. Within each specific step, I had a timetable. The process was comprehensive.

Then one day my eyes were opened. I realized my goals were established on human terms, with human ambition and human pride. In fact my goals probably were in conflict with the goals God wanted for my life. I tossed aside the planning book and started to live by faith, allowing God to lead me and God to provide. Each day I attempted to be productive and to achieve according to what each day brought. I was always excited about a new day.

Currently I use a weekly planner. I list work projects required for the week, and I list to-do tasks around the house. When I complete a project or task, I proudly check it off the list. If I complete a project not on the list, of course I add it to the list and then proudly check it off. Remember, I am an accountant.

GREATER AND LESSER

A final thought on worry is that Jesus speaks of the greater and the lesser. The lesser creatures are birds and flowers; the greater creatures are humans. The argument goes like this: if God takes interest in the lesser creatures, then God will provide for the greater creatures. If a sacred life is born as a baby, and God cherishes each child, then will He not sustain and provide for the cherished child? If God created the earth, the heavens, the seas, and all that is in them, and exclaimed that His creation was good, then will He not sustain and provide for the earth?

The earth spins. According to the laws of physics, an object in motion eventually slows down due to friction and other forces. Why is it that the earth does not slow down, even when we test its rate of spin with atomic clocks? God sustains the earth. He will sustain you if you will believe and trust him. When a challenge or problem comes our way, we should respond in absolute faith, saying "I wonder how God will help solve this problem?" When faith in God increases, then worry decreases.

CHAPTER THIRTEEN

SOCIALISM, CONTROL, AND THE TWO KINGDOMS

SOCIALISM

Terrence Ball describes socialism as a social and economic doctrine that calls for public rather than private ownership or control of property and natural resources. According to the socialist view, individuals do not live or work in isolation. They live in cooperation with one another. Furthermore, everything that people produce is in some sense a social product, and everyone who contributes to the production of a good is entitled to a share in it. Society as a whole, therefore, should own or at least control property for the benefit of all its members.[1]

Ball continues:

> This conviction puts socialism in opposition to capitalism, which is based on private ownership of the means of production and allows individual choices in a free market to determine how goods and services are distributed. Socialists complain

that capitalism necessarily leads to unfair and exploitative concentrations of wealth and power in the hands of the relative few who emerge victorious from free-market competition—people who then use their wealth and power to reinforce their dominance in society. Because such people are rich, they may choose where and how to live, and their choices in turn limit the options of the poor. As a result, terms such as *individual freedom* and *equality of opportunity* may be meaningful for capitalists but can only ring hollow for working people, who must do the capitalists' bidding if they are to survive.[2]

The important point is that socialism uses social ownership, which can be public, collective, cooperative, or of equity. In America, socialism is *private* ownership but *government* control.

The reach of governments, both local and federal, is so vast that socialism in America is government control over private ownership. In fact, with the stroke of a pen, the president can stop a multibillion-dollar investment by private industries to build a pipeline from Canada through America. This act results in the laying off of thousands of workers, incredible losses to businesses, and energy availability becoming jeopardized in the future. This is a demonstration of incredible power to subvert democracy, eliminate freedom of enterprise, cause loss to private investment on private land, and bypass Congress. It is a dramatic display of a powerful king in a totalitarian regime.

Government controls everything with endless commissions, agencies, committees, and courts. Personal freedoms are reduced by requiring permits, zoning restrictions, registration fees, taxation, and other roadblocks to free enterprise. Socialism is not just public ownership—in America, it is government control over private property.

Here is a recent example of power exercised through an agency and an example of practical communism. The Center for Disease Control (CDC) issued mandates to stop economic activity in order to stop the spread of the SARS-CoV-2 coronavirus. Among the gatherings they sought to stop or limit were church services, schools, and sporting contests. How can a single person, as the head of an agency, climb to such power?

This power of government-appointed officials is the thrust of socialism, which leads to communism.

Going forward, our country will be socialist and under practical communism, ruled by Washington, DC, elites making decisions based on bribes from political action committees for the purpose of retaining power by any means.

Why do socialists and communists hate Christianity? One reason is that practicing Christians defy the wrong laws of government, which are contrary to the laws of God. The book of Acts tells of the apostle Peter being brought before the elders for healing a blind man in the name of Jesus. They hated Peter for this good deed. Peter displayed the power of Jesus in this miracle. They commanded him to be silent about Jesus. Peter became bold and defiant, saying to the assembly that God would judge whether it was better to listen to the elders or to God (see Acts 4:18-20). Peter pledged to speak of what he knew and had seen.

Christians must be persecuted completely in order to fulfill humanistic, materialistic, and authoritarian pursuits. Jesus prophesied this hatred. The gospel of John says that everyone practicing evil hates the light. Such evildoers do not come to the light because their deeds would be exposed (see Jn 3:19–20). The call today for transparency in government transactions will expose corruption.

How can God work a financial miracle in such a situation? Financial miracles are from the intervention of God, who responds to prayer in accordance with His will. Individual practicing Christians may still receive financial miracles. However, our national integrity is out of bounds for a national financial miracle.

Robert Schumacher in an article in the Christian Post writes as follows:

> When you tell an adherent of one of these belief systems and their oppressive government that their actions or ideas are wrong, it produces an egocentric rage that quickly manifests in authoritarian actions that first move to silence such "hate speech" and then go further to squash the persons themselves. The Bible says we shouldn't be surprised at this kind of aggression because the mind and behavior governed by the flesh and the world is hostile to God; it does not submit to God's law, nor can it do so (Rom 8:7).
>
> The natural outworking of this, from a governance standpoint, is the rejection and outlawing of liberties and freedoms of the general public. In rejecting God, tyrannical governments and their underlying worldviews suppress the fact that God is a free being, and since we are made in His likeness, we are also free beings who have innate freedoms that naturally flow to us from our Creator.
>
> And for authoritarian governments, that just can't be allowed.[3]

We will soon be in a situation similar to that reported in the book of Judges where each person will do what is right in his own eyes.

RETURNING TO GOD

In the book of Judges, the people return to God only when a crisis occurs and there is widespread suffering and distress. There was suffering and distress during the depression of 2008, but there did not appear to be a surge of individuals returning to church. Individual and family suffering was reduced by Congress extending unemployment benefits for up to ninety-nine weeks in some states.

After the terrorists' acts of 9/11 against the World Trade Center in New York City, the Pentagon, and Flight 93, the nation returned to God for a short period of time.

The Gallup, Inc. reported on March 29, 2021, that US church membership fell below 50 percent for first time:

> Americans' membership in houses of worship continued to decline last year, dropping below 50% for the first time in Gallup's eight-decade trend. In 2020, 47% of Americans said they belonged to a church, synagogue or mosque, down from 50% in 2018 and 70% in 1999.
>
> U.S. church membership was 73% when Gallup first measured it in 1937 and remained near 70% for the next six decades, before beginning a steady decline around the turn of the 21st century.
>
> The decline in church membership is primarily a function of the increasing number of Americans who express no religious preference. Over the past two decades, the percentage of Americans who do not identify with any religion has grown from 8% in 1998-2000 to 13% in 2008-2010 and 21% over the past three years.[4]

What event or catastrophe will cause the people to return to God again?

DEMANDING A KING

At one time the nation of Israel in the Old Testament had individual freedoms. There was no formal government. Each person was restrained by their adherence to the Law of Moses as a check on their behavior. To atone for sinful acts, they used sacrifices of animals and grain to seek God's forgiveness and favor.

At one point, the people demanded to have a king like other nations. Read the abbreviated discussion concerning the matter with the prophet Samuel (see 1 Sm 8:1–22). This is the outcome of communism and totalitarianism.

When the prophet Samuel was old, he appointed his sons as judges over Israel. But the sons were corrupt and received dishonest gain. The people demanded a king to rule over them. This request displeased Samuel, since God was the ruler over the nation with administration by the priests, according to the Law of Moses. So Samuel prayed to God, who answered that the people had not rejected Samuel; they had rejected God. God recounted the bad deeds the people had committed, including worshipping other gods. God told Samuel to let them have a king as they wished.

The prophet Samuel made these points about the behavior of a king:

- He would take their sons and appoint them for his own chariots and to be his horsemen.
- He would appoint captains over his thousands, would set some to plow his ground and reap his harvest, and would set others to make his weapons of war.
- He would take their daughters to be perfumers, cooks, and bakers.
- He would take the best of their fields, vineyards, and olive groves and give them to his servants.
- He would take a tenth of their grain and give it to his officers and servants.

- He would take their male servants, female servants, finest young men, and donkeys and put them to his work.
- He would take a tenth of their sheep.
- And they would be his servants.

It seems to me that people who desire to have a king, with socialism and government control, presume that their battles will be fought by others and not themselves. They believe their wages will be guaranteed without competitive reviews, that retirement plans will be always available, that poor investment returns will be guaranteed by the government, that medical benefits will be available, that maternity benefits will be available, that child care will be available, and that there will be free education, including college.

In summary, people think socialism will make life easier, with less work, less risk, and more free time. It is a self-interested, selfish proposition.

However, as scripture says, the king will take from you and not give to you. The majority will always oppress the minority. In the case of socialism, the ruling class will always oppress the working class.

In addition, the people who desire socialism have rejected God as a provider. They have put their trust in a group of sinful men and women who think of only themselves. This group keeps itself in power by passing laws benefiting themselves and their contributors. The government will lord it over you.

God has been replaced by government. Personal restraint through following the Ten Commandments is gone. Sin is not recognized. God will just leave us to our own devices for self-destruction. God will not provide financial miracles. He will allow us to suffer until we return to God. America is on the road to socialism and moving away from God.

The founders of America stood firm on values different from all other nations of the world. These values include God, charity, individualism, freedom of choice, self-governance, personal property rights, fairness, freedom to work, freedom of religion, justice, judgment by peers, and other liberties.

THE END GAME

The end game is not advancing in a worldly kingdom, but preparing for a spiritual kingdom. The Christian understands salvation is from God through faith in Jesus Christ, and this salvation has nothing to do with worldly circumstances or governments. Salvation is a miracle of love and the grace of God accepting us individually and forgiving our sins. It is by God's grace providing us salvation, even though we deserve punishment and hell. It is through faith and not works that we bring salvation into our lives. Faith is a gift from God (see Eph 2:8).

Christians live under many types of rulers and governments: kings, dictators, and dictated national religions like Islam, Buddhism, Hinduism, and New Age religions. The end game for Christians stands firm and assured.

This great assurance is spelled out in a marvelous passage of scripture, Romans 8:35–39. Paul, the apostle used by God to deliver God's message, experienced numerous trials and physical persecutions. He says that nothing can separate us from the love of God. Tribulations, distress, persecution, famine, nakedness, peril, and the sword cannot separate us from the love of God in Christ Jesus. Even when these things, which include financial persecution, happen and become part of our daily suffering, we are more than conquerors through Him who loved us. "For I am persuaded that neither death nor life, nor angels nor principalities nor powers, nor things present nor things to come, nor height nor depth, nor any other created thing, shall be able to separate us from the love of God which is in Christ Jesus our Lord" (Rom 8:38–39 NKJV).

In the midst of government persecution, corruption, and

scandal, God through Jesus Christ will watch over us. In the gospel of John, there is a visual expression of Jesus as the shepherd and His disciples as sheep. They hear His voice and follow Him, knowing all their cares are satisfied. The sheep are secure and at peace. Jesus says that He gives them eternal life, and they shall never perish. Neither shall anyone snatch them out of His hand. Jesus also proclaims that He and His Father are one (see Jn 10:27–30).

Therefore there is full assurance that our financial challenges and suffering will pass, and eternal love and life will be upon us.

FINANCIAL MIRACLES

How does a financial miracle fit into a socialist or communist system? Jesus lived under the dictatorship of the Roman Empire, with appointed and dedicated rulers of territories.

The answer is that there are two kingdoms: the kingdom of God and the kingdom of humanity, which is an earthly kingdom. Jesus lived in both kingdoms, and practicing Christians live in both kingdoms also. The kingdom of God is a spiritual kingdom that one cannot see. The kingdom of humanity is a physical kingdom that can be seen.

The kingdom of God includes repentance and believing the gospel message. In order to receive a financial miracle, one must live in the kingdom of God and also be a good citizen in the human kingdom. One does this by following the just laws of the earthly kingdom, insofar as those laws do not override the laws of God.

When a government overrides the laws of God, the freedoms of Christians and the Christion religion are challenged. We are alert to the destructive nature of laws that pull people away from God to their own perdition. Such ungodly lawmakers and their political followers are only involved in the worldly kingdom and will not be acceptable into the godly kingdom.

CHAPTER FOURTEEN

LIVING IN THE KINGDOM OF GOD

HOW DOES ONE ENTER THE KINGDOM OF GOD?

The writers for the organization The People of the Book have an easy-to-understand description of how to enter the kingdom of God, starting with a scriptural foundation: "Now after John was put in prison, Jesus came to Galilee, preaching the gospel of the kingdom of God, and saying, 'The time is fulfilled, and the kingdom of God is at hand. Repent, and believe in the gospel'" (Mk 1:14–15 NKJV). Here is the explanation:

REPENT– Recognize your sin and desire to turn from it (Mt 4:17; Pr 28:13).

- This includes an awareness of being totally unworthy to enter (Mt 5:3).
- This includes an awareness of being totally inadequate to enter (Mt 5:6).
- This awareness produces a sense of shame (Ge 3:10).

BELIEVE THE GOSPEL- Trust in the Lord Jesus Christ for your salvation (Jn 3:16-18; Rom 10:9-11; Eph 2:8-9; 1 Cor 15:1-8).

- Jesus is the only way (Jn 14:6).
- It is necessary to count the cost (Lk 14:25-33; Lk 9:23-26; Lk 9:62; Lk 18:28-30; Ac 14:22).
- One must come to Jesus in helpless, trusting dependence (Mt 18:3).
- Jesus' death provides for the forgiveness of sins (Mt 26:26-29; Eph 1:7; Ac 13:32-39).
- Jesus rose from the dead and offers eternal life to all those who believe in Him (Jn 11:25-27).
- Jesus is Lord and God (Jn 8:24).
- There must be a conscious decision to enter through the narrow gate (Mt 7:13-14).
- The evidence of true faith and legitimate entrance into the kingdom is demonstrated by obedience (Mt 7:21) and the fruit of a transformed life (2 Cor 5:17).

Many who think they are in the kingdom of God, are not in the kingdom at all (Mt 7:22-23; Lk 13:22-30; 1 Cor 6:9-11; Gal 5:19-21).[1]

Remember, we cannot enter the kingdom on our own power. The Holy Spirit leads us and provides us with a new birth, giving us power for daily living, such as cleaner language, stronger desire to serve others, and stronger desire to praise God with our lives. In our new lives of faith, we desire to use the means of grace, including preaching of the Word, baptism, and Holy Communion.

Financial miracles are available to those living in the kingdom of God.

In the gospel of Mark, there was a situation in which children wanted to come to Jesus but the disciples made them stay away, thinking they were too young and lacking understanding to be taught. When Jesus saw this, He was displeased. He said that the kingdom of God was made up of such as these young children, and we must receive the kingdom of God as a child or we cannot enter (see Mk 10:14–15).

How do we receive the kingdom of God like a child? Think about the attributes of a child, and you can answer this question by yourselves. Children can be in the kingdom.

Another barrier to the kingdom is riches. "Then Jesus looked around and said to His disciples, 'How hard it is for those who have riches to enter the kingdom of God!'" (Mk 10:23 NKJV).

Another barrier is looking for the kingdom and when it will come. "Now when He was asked by the Pharisees when the kingdom of God would come, He answered them and said, 'The kingdom of God does not come with observation; nor will they say, "See here!" or "See there!" For indeed, the kingdom of God is within you'" (Lk 17:20–21 NKJV).

Another barrier to entry into the kingdom is that we must be born again. "Jesus answered, 'Most assuredly, I say to you, unless one is born of water and the Spirit, he cannot enter the kingdom of God'" (Jn 3:5 NKJV).

CHAPTER FIFTEEN

FINANCIAL CARES AND THE SPIRITUALLY POOR

THE DECEITFULNESS OF WEALTH

Some may think a financial miracle will make them rich, and the purpose of a financial miracle is wealth creation. A financial miracle produced or directed by God cannot go against the nature of God. Only Satan would provide a financial miracle that would ultimately do damage or hurt the beneficiary.

Remember the moral attributes of God: God is righteous and affirms what is right as opposed to what is wrong. God is holy. *Holiness* refers to moral excellence, which God demands of His children and which He supplies. God is love. God loved and suffered by giving His life on the cross for the redemption of humanity, desiring good for all His creatures (see Gn 1:31; Ps 145:9; Mk 10:18).

God is truth. All truth, whether natural, physical, or religious, is grounded in God. God is wisdom, which means doing the best thing in the best way at the best time for the best purpose (see 1 Tm 1:17).

Providing salvation for God's children is the ultimate goal. Sometimes a financial miracle would provide harm to His children, just as it would when a loving father gives too much cash to an immature, selfish, and unthankful son. Remember the story of the Prodigal Son, who squandered the father's inheritance in a faraway country? (See Lk 15:11–31). The Prodigal Son realized that his father's servants were treated well. Therefore it was better to be a servant of his father than to continue as he was living. So he left for home.

Jesus told a parable about a farmer sowing seed in four types of soil. The soil types were by the wayside, on stony places, among thorns, and on good soil. The seed is the Word of the kingdom of God, the farmer is God, and the soil represents four types of people hearing the Word of God.

Jesus provided an explanation of the results in Matthew 13:18–23. The following is a summary of that explanation.

Jesus said that when one hears the message and does not understand it, then the wicked one takes away what was planted in the listener's heart. This is the soil by the wayside. The stony field is one who receives the Word with gladness but has no firm foundation. Therefore, when persecution comes, the listener falls and does not stand firm. The seed among thorns is one who hears the Word, but the cares of the world and the deceitfulness of money stop the Word from growing. The listener becomes unfruitful and distracted. The good soil is one who hears the Word, understands it, and is productive, bearing fruit, some a hundredfold and some a lesser amount.

Our discussion involves Matthew 13:22 the people who received the seeds among thorns. They hear the Word with joy, but the cares of this world and the deceitfulness of riches choke the Word. What is the deceitfulness of riches? *Merriam-Webster's Dictionary* defines *deceit* as the act of causing someone to accept as true or valid what is false or invalid: the act or practice of deceiving; deception, or achieving one's goals through a web of deceit. Albert Barnes discusses the image of thorns.

These represent the cares, the anxieties, and the deceitful lure of riches, or the way in which a DESIRE to be rich deceives people.

They take the time and attention. They do not leave opportunity to examine the state of the soul. Besides, riches allure, and promise what they do not yield. They promise to make us happy; but, when gained, they do not do it. The soul is not satisfied. There is the same desire to possess more wealth. And to this there is no end "but death." In doing it there is every temptation to be dishonest, to cheat, to take advantage of others, to oppress others, and to wring their hard earnings from the poor. Every evil passion is therefore cherished by the love of gain; and it is no wonder that the word is choked, and every good feeling destroyed, by this "execrable love of gold" How many, O how many, thus foolishly drown themselves in destruction and perdition! How many more might reach heaven, if it were not for this deep-seated love of that which fills the mind with care, deceives the soul, and finally leaves it naked, and guilty, and lost![1]

Matthew Henry has a further explanation about the deceitfulness of riches including insight into the complacency of wealth. Complacency of wealth is where the wealthy are fully satisfied in the way things are without attempting to make things better.

Those who, by their care and industry, have raised estates, and so the danger that arises from care seems to be over, and they continue hearers of the word, yet are still in a snare (Jer 5:4-5); it is hard for them to enter into the kingdom of heaven: they are apt to promise themselves that in riches which is not in them; to rely upon them, and to take an inordinate complacency in them; and this chokes the word as much as care did. Observe, it is not so much riches, as the deceitfulness of riches that does the mischief: now they cannot be said to be deceitful to us unless we put our confidence in them, and raise our expectations from them, and then it is that they choke the good seed.[2]

A MIRACLE FOR THE RICH

Many people might think that the rich do not have need to request a financial miracle. However, many millionaires request financial miracles because a business deal has gone south, the projected sales do not appear, the leveraged buyout cannot pay the debt, the IRS initiates an audit, or a divorce happens that splits the assets.

The tragedy is that money has replaced God in the lives of the rich. The rich depend on and trust their wealth. They look to money for help when problems arise. They attempt to settle differences by a financial payment. They fire those with different opinions. They exercise authority and power over the poor. They bribe political partners in order to secure government contracts. The deceitfulness of riches moves them to perdition.

Jesus said that it is very difficult for a rich man to come into the kingdom of heaven. He compared that struggle with the struggle of a camel to go through the eye of a needle—which is impossible (see Mt 19:23-24). Lord, help us to detach our riches from our hearts.

Remember, wealth alone is not the sin. The sin lies in dependence and trust in wealth coupled with the continuing desire for more. A financial miracle from God cannot happen in this environment.

MIDDLE AMERICA

People may say, "This information does not apply to me because I am not wealthy. I am part of Middle America." However, the lure of better things—a college savings account, a nicer car, clothes with fancy labels, shoes with a checkmark, and other things—this lure is deep inside all of us. It is a deceptive lure. We are never satisfied, always thinking, always plotting, and always looking for a way to make ourselves better than others. We are never in a state of contentment, never at peace with ourselves, and never satisfied. We are restless.

Remember the statement by St. Augustine of Hippo: "You have made us for yourself, O Lord, and our heart is restless until it rests in you."[3]

The financial problem occurs very subtly. One slips into debt, consumer debt, the kind of debt with a monthly payment, the kind with an outrageous interest rate that one is not aware of even though it is posted. The things purchased have a short useful life. Credit cards allow us to spend money we do not have for things we do not need. Scripture tells us to live within our means.

John the Baptist preached that every tree that does not bear good fruit is cut down and thrown into the fire. The people asked for direction. John the Baptist responded to the soldiers, saying that they should not intimidate anyone with the strength of the sword or accuse falsely. He also said to be content with one's wages. In our day the sword is not used. We use the courts, where a person can be threatened with a lawsuit. Or we engage in public thrashings in the media, in order to coerce the helpless man into compliance (see Lk 3:14).

Being content with our wages and living within our means is always a challenge. Rather than using up old things and doing without, we buy on credit. The credit balance builds with outrageous interest added, to the point where we miss payments. At the same time, the things we bought need fixing. The pay raise we are expecting falls through. The Christmas bonus does not come. We are stressed and need a vacation. The vacation is great, but we are now thousands of dollars deeper in debt.

We pray to God for a financial miracle. What does God do? God allows suffering in order to teach us a lesson. The lesson is to watch out for the deceitfulness of wealth. Return to the Lord, your God. Repent of sinful spending and believe the gospel. With your next purchase, can you say that God will bless this purchase? Will this purchase glorify God?

Our relationship with money needs to change. This change is in the heart, which should be a new heart with a new trust in God for our livelihood. We leave trust in wealth, position, authority, degrees, and government behind. We are unshackled from the desire for more, and we are free.

SPIRITUALLY POOR

Scripture talks about the "spiritually poor" (see Mt 5:3) as a description of the heart. To be spiritually poor is to have no righteousness in ourselves, to understand our sinfulness, to know helplessness, to depend on God and His mercy, and to be humble in our tasks. The opposite is arrogance, pride, and prestige. Remember, Jesus said that He came to bring good news to the poor.

We live in two kingdoms: the spiritual kingdom and the worldly kingdom. The kingdom of God is a spiritual kingdom. It is alive and moving among us, even though it is not recognized. Sadly, most individuals are not concerned about the status of their souls and where they will spend eternity, because they are busy depending on their own efforts to survive.

Jesus Christ knows the heart. He judges the heart as to which kingdom has the greater influence over one's day-to-day activities.

The spiritually poor are closer to a blessed or happy state than the rich. Riches produce care and fear of losing them. Jesus says that the poor in spirit receive the kingdom of heaven (see Mt 5:3).

To be poor is to be in need. In the world, we see the needs of the poor vividly on television and in the news. Nations send humanitarian aid to help in times of disaster and calamity. This is the state of being worldly poor—without resources, without electricity, without clean water, without clean homes, without nutrition, without safety, without medical facilities and so on.

Contrast the needs of the worldly kingdom with the needs of the spiritual kingdom. Individuals have needs in the spiritual kingdom, including understanding truth, receiving righteousness, understanding the forgiveness of sin, understanding service to others, receiving contentment without money, loving your enemies, forgiving people who trespass against you, separating the heart from clinging to wealth, desiring worship, desiring to participate in the sacraments, desiring to pray to God through Jesus Christ, desiring to honor marriage and children, desiring to serve others, and so on.

Martin Luther explains our relationship with possessions:

> We are not to run away from property, house, home, wife, and children, wandering around the countryside as a burden to other people… [instead, this] is what it means: In our heart we should be able to leave house and home, wife and children. Even though we continue to live among them, eating with them and serving them out of love, as God has commanded, still we should be able, if necessary, to give them up at any time for God's sake. If you are able to do this, you have forsaken everything, in the sense that your heart is not taken captive but remains pure of greed and of dependence, trust, and confidence in anything. A rich man may properly be called "spiritually poor" without discarding his possessions.[4]

This new relationship to money and possessions is what I call the "New Financial Nature". It comes to us from the Holy Spirit, and is one of the final steps in becoming a Christian. Remember the SCARF method of coming to Christ?

- S: understanding and recognizing *sin* in our lives
- C: Jesus *Christ* died for our sins
- A: *and* now what
- R: *repent* of our sins
- F: live by *faith*

Living by faith brings along the Holy Spirit, who provides a new heart, changing every relationship one experiences, including marriage, children, work, worship, service, and money.

After restoring our relationships and becoming Christians, we can receive power to make proper, godly decisions about money. We can experience daily miracles, understanding each new breath is a gift from God. We can experience financial miracles, including contentment with the things we have and recognition of the opportunities God provides.

———— ✦ ————

CHAPTER SIXTEEN

GOD KNOWS OUR THOUGHTS AND SITUATION

GOD KNOWS

You may be in deep internal turmoil concerning the state of your financial affairs. You may face heavyhearted decisions that require you to analyze, explore, and understand the effects of financial choices on your children, spouse, and household workload.

As we project into the future, the unknown, we often enter the spiritual world and pray fervently to God for help. But our cry for help may appear to go unanswered, leaving us questioning if God knows our situation, our struggle, our confusion, or our inability to sort out what is most important.

We ask for financial miracles, but our suffering increases. In frustration, we ask whether God understands that we are not making it. Listen to a psalm of David:

> How long, O LORD? Will You forget me forever?
> How long will You hide Your face from me?

> How long shall I take counsel in my soul, *Having*
> sorrow in my heart daily? How long will my
> enemy be exalted over me? (Ps 13:1–2 NKJV).

You are not alone in your cry for help. God is fully aware of our situations. He allows us to make decisions in an attempt to provide ourselves relief, decisions based on godly insight and influence. Below are some scripture passages that prove from the Word of God that God knows each of us, loves each of us, and knows about our situations.

In one psalm, the palmist says God has searched him and knows him when he sits down and when he gets up. God understands his thoughts and is acquainted with his daily routine. God knows his speech and language. God has His hand upon him. The psalmist questions where he can go from God's spirit or run from God's presence (see Ps 139:1–7).

> Are not two sparrows sold for a copper coin? And
> not one of them falls to the ground apart from
> your Father's will. But the very hairs of your head
> are all numbered. Do not fear therefore; you are
> of more value than many sparrows (Mt 10:29–31
> NKJV).

Financial miracles are available to those who desire to know God the Father and the Son, Jesus Christ, and to watch for the leading of the Holy Spirit. The leading of the Holy Spirit is a way God provides financial miracles. Financial miracles contain a human element, such as running into an old friend who makes work time available, or finding an emergency supply of parts through a telephone conversation. I recall a contractor building our house who prayed aloud, "Lord, send me a bricklayer."

In another instance, one year the tax law changes were widespread, stretching my firm's capability beyond the limit. An old tax preparer friend came to the office unexpectedly, and we hired him to supplement our accounting staff. This was a financial miracle.

God knows all about us and the desires of our hearts.

THINKING

Jesus knows our thoughts. According to the Ten Commandments, it is not only the evil we do that is sin; it is also the good we do *not* do that is sin. It is also the thinking about evil that is sin. Our thoughts are not hidden from Jesus.

Jesus knows us and the thoughts in our hearts, so He knows our stressors, our anxieties, our problems, our dilemmas, our inner struggles, and our desires. Jesus desires to provide for us when accomplishing God's purpose.

There are several passages from the Bible in which the gospel writers saw Jesus in action, reading the thoughts of people. In one passage, a paralytic was brought to Jesus, lying on a bed. Several individuals carry him in to Jesus. Their action is a demonstration of faith. Jesus saw their faith and told the paralytic to be of good cheer, because his sins were forgiven. Religious leaders thought in their hearts that Jesus was blasphemous, because only God could forgive sins. Knowing their thoughts, Jesus told them that the Son of Man—a phrase He often used to describe Himself—had power on earth to forgive sin. Jesus told the paralytic to arise, take up his bed, and go home (see Mt 9:2–4).

"For the wisdom of this world is foolishness with God. For it is written, *'He catches the wise in their own craftiness';* and again, *'The LORD knows the thoughts of the wise, that they are futile'"* (1 Cor 3:19–20 NKJV). The point is that Jesus knows us thoroughly, even our thoughts. Sometimes He will push into our heads a thought for action.

A friend of mine at church, an elderly lady, told me of a time when she received the thought to call a person. The thought would not leave her. She rationalized that she really did not know the person nor what to say to her. Nevertheless the thought continued until she called the person. The person was having a stroke and needed assistance.

THE FOUR THOUSAND

The Lord thinks of us and has compassion on us before we ourselves understand our situation and need. This is demonstrated through the miracle of the feeding of the four thousand. While praying earnestly and fervently for a financial miracle, we might be thankful for the hidden solution already in the works.

The story of the feeding of the four thousand is from Mark 8:1–3. A multitude of people followed Jesus for several days and had nothing to eat. Jesus called His disciples to Him and said that He had compassion on the people. He said that if He sent them away, some of the people would faint, since there were elderly people in the crowd.

Martin Luther comments:

> Here tell me, if the multitude had sent an embassy to Christ to report on their need, could they have formulated their report as well as Christ himself here thinks it out and holds it before his disciples? For how would they or could they paint it better or allege stronger reasons to move him, than to have said: Oh, beloved Lord, have compassion on the poor multitude of people, men, women and children, who have followed thee so far in order to hear thee? In the second place, consider that they have now remained and continued with thee for three days. In the third place, remember that they have nothing to eat and are in the desert. In the fourth place, if you send them away fasting they

must faint on the way before they arrive home, especially the weak men and the women and children. In the fifth place, consider also that some have come far, etc. Behold, Christ reflected upon all this himself before anyone speaks with him and has himself formed the prayer so beautifully in his own heart. Yes, he is distressed on their account before they think of praying to him, and earnestly discussed with the disciples their need and gave counsel what to do in their behalf. ...

What then is all this but a purely living sermon, proving and witnessing that Christ is so earnestly and heartily concerned about us, and before we can propose anything to him, he looks into our hearts better than we ourselves can, so that no mortal person could speak with another more heartily. For he does not wait for someone to say to him: Oh, Lord, have compassion on the multitude, think how they have held out, how far they are from home, etc. Yes, he says, I have compassion on them already and have thought over it all before.[1]

Jesus has compassion on us and knows our needs before we pray to request help. A financial miracle to solve a dilemma may be in the works. God gathers the necessary individuals, moves their hearts to compassion, provides tools to make things happen, and, at the same time, satisfies the needs of several people.

We come to Jesus in helplessness. Perhaps we lack a truthful partner, support, or the strength to handle our many financial challenges and anxieties. There is no place to receive financial confidence tied together with honor, integrity, uprightness, and righteousness. We do not have the strength to fight against the temptations of government, cheats, manipulation, and bad actors.

We finally relax our guard, submit our will, stop fighting, and surrender to the One who can turn our lives around: Jesus.

We admit the great sinfulness of unbelief. We understand that the Son of God, sinless, received the wrath of God. He was scourged, mocked, and executed on the cross, substituting Himself for the wrath we deserved. We repent of our sins and turn our lives in a new direction. We receive the gifts of faith to believe and the Holy Spirit for the amendment of our sinful lives. We begin lives of faith, putting ourselves in front of the means of grace by way of baptism, Holy Communion, preaching, and the Bible.

The result is that we are born again with a new worldview, new language, new thanksgiving, new forgiveness, new relationships, new honesty, and new life. This powerful and confident life includes working to please God (not for money) and working to serve others (not yourself). It includes financial integrity, patience, trust, forgiveness, acceptance of loss, acceptance of defeat, and the drive to help others—even those who wish you harm.

This change is the "New Financial Nature".

CHAPTER SEVENTEEN

DIVINE PROVIDENCE AND THE AFFAIRS OF NATIONS

DIVINE PROVIDENCE

Providence is the continuous activity of God in His creation, by which He preserves and governs. The doctrine of providence affirms God's absolute lordship over His creation and confirms the dependence of all creation on the Creator. It is denial of the idea that the universe is governed by chance or fate.[1]

God can accomplish a financial miracle by ordering the activities of men and leading them according to the directions of Jesus. What is amazing about the example below is that Jesus knew the movement of the man carrying a jug of water. That was an unusual activity, since women usually fetched water. Jesus knew where they would meet up, knew where the man would return, and knew what to say to the owner of the room.

> Then came the Day of Unleavened Bread, when the Passover must be killed. And He sent Peter and John, saying, "Go and prepare the Passover

for us, that we may eat." So they said to Him, "Where do You want us to prepare?" And He said to them, "Behold, when you have entered the city, a man will meet you carrying a pitcher of water; follow him into the house which he enters. Then you shall say to the master of the house, 'The Teacher says to you, "Where is the guest room where I may eat the Passover with My disciples?"' Then he will show you a large, furnished upper room; there make ready" (Lk 22:7-12 NKJV).

Matthew Henry comments on this miracle:

He directed those whom he employed whither they should go (v. 9, 10): they must follow a man bearing a pitcher of water, and he must be their guide to the house. Christ could have described the house to them; probably it was a house they knew, and he might have said no more than, Go to such a one's house, or to a house in such a street, with such a sign, etc. But he directed them thus, to teach them to depend upon the conduct of Providence, and to follow that, step by step. They went, not knowing whither they went, nor whom they followed. Being come to the house, they must desire the master of the house to show them a room (v. 11), and he will readily do it, (v. 12). Whether it was a friend's house or a public house does not appear; but the disciples found their guide, and the house, and the room, just as he had said to them (v. 13); for they need not fear a disappointment who go upon Christ's word; according to the orders given them, they got everything in readiness for the Passover, v. 11."[2]

Jesus knows where you are each day and can direct your path by thoughts or signs, if you allow Him. It is an incredible thought that Jesus knows my whereabouts. He is omniscient, knowing everything, having unlimited knowledge, having infinite awareness.

I was driving on the interstate system heading from Columbus toward Indianapolis, using a global positioning system (GPS) to direct me. I suddenly became aware that perhaps fifty cars around me were using the same system. The system knew exactly where the car was, knew my future destination, knew the next turn I needed to make, knew how many feet in front of me a stop sign was, and knew how to correct me if I made a wrong turn. This same knowledge was available to every car around me in the same nice lady's voice.

If humans, with limited ability, can create a system with this unbelievable knowledge of my whereabouts, then God can certainly know where I am, what I am doing, and what I am thinking. God knows me. He is aware of my needs. He has the intention of loving me and helping me resolve my prayers.

If we pay attention and study the activities and interactions of the people around us, we can notice the financial miracles. We appreciate a kernel of corn dying in the ground and then producing a crop of great yield.

Jesus may need an empty room at some point. We should be prepared for Him to use us and our property as He pleases. This same concept goes for an emergency fund: a fund of money one keeps available for unforeseen needs. That need may be an emergency experienced by someone else in the body of Christ, not only one's own. Sharing one's emergency fund results in a financial miracle to someone.

"Divine providence" is a term used by many people to disclose who is supporting their family or organization. Divine providence makes available income sources, provides financial miracles in their midst, and changes hearts to become compassionate listeners and givers.

Here is an example of divine providence working with the poor and destitute through the Shekhinah Clinic in Tamale, Ghana, West Africa. The Shekhinah Clinic for the Poor and Destitute was officially established in March 1991 by Dr. David Abdulai Fuseini, popularly known as Dr. Choggu or "the Mad Doctor."

The witness to divine providence is written on their website, together with their vision statement and mission statement:

> Shekhinah Clinic for the Poor and Destitute, since we opened our doors has had no regular source of funding outside Divine Providence. Every day is a gift and every day we witness one miracle after another... for the past 25 years. We depend on occasional and spontaneous donations, individuals who are passionate to our mission and vision as well as organizations both within and outside Ghana.
>
> The Vision statement
> Shekhinah clinic for the poor and destitute aspires to be a source of light, hope and joy for the poorest of the poor in the society in order that they may experience God's unconditional love.
>
> The Mission statement
> Shekhinah clinic for the poor and Destitute exists to provide services medical care, shelter, meal, clothing and other support services to the poorest of the poor freely and unconditionally purely for the love of God and Neighbor and depending solely on Divine Providence.[3]

THE AFFAIRS OF NATIONS

Divine providence controls the affairs of nations under God's total sovereignty. God is King over all the nations, doing what He wills to accomplish His purpose.

Do you remember the Declaration of Independence of the United States of America? In the closing paragraph, they state that support for their decision is based on divine providence. This, of course, was a life-threatening decision. They were facing the great British fleet plus mercenaries. Nevertheless the people pledged in earnest and with determination "our Lives, our Fortunes and our sacred Honor" with "a firm reliance on the protection of divine Providence":

> We, therefore, the Representatives of the united States of America, in General Congress, Assembled, appealing to the Supreme Judge of the world for the rectitude of our intentions, do, in the Name, and by Authority of the good People of these Colonies, solemnly publish and declare, That these United Colonies are, and of Right ought to be Free and Independent States; that they are Absolved from all Allegiance to the British Crown, and that all political connection between them and the State of Great Britain, is and ought to be totally dissolved; and that as Free and Independent States, they have full Power to levy War, conclude Peace, contract Alliances, establish Commerce, and to do all other Acts and Things which Independent States may of right do. And for the support of this Declaration, with a firm reliance on the protection of divine Providence, we mutually pledge to each other our Lives, our Fortunes and our sacred Honor.

God's divine providence and control over the nations can be demonstrated using His favorite nation of Israel, which was held in bondage for four hundred years before God brought them out of Egypt. He did so with amazement and a mighty hand, using plagues of common elements (water, frogs, gnats, flies, livestock, boils, hail, locusts, darkness, and firstborn offspring). God made a distinction between the Egyptians and the Israelites, such that God's favored nation did not suffer from several plagues.

God can use ungodly nations to do His will. An example is when God used Caesar Augustus to bring Mary and Joseph to the city of Bethlehem in order to fulfill the prophecy of Micah that "out of you shall come forth to Me The One to be Ruler in Israel" (Micah 5:2 NKJV). God accomplished this by the order of Caesar Augustus to hold a census requiring everyone to go his own city. The timing of the decree was marvelous in that Mary was due while in Bethlehem, and the baby was delivered. In addition, the inn was full, providing us an example of the humility of God coming into our midst (see Lk 2:1–5).

The point is that God can work with, lead, help, care for, and sustain the nations. Without His providence, the world would not exist. The call for us to seek the face of God, turning from our wicked ways, continues to this day. God offers forgiveness of sins and healing of the land (see 2 Chr 7:14).

CHAPTER EIGHTEEN

COMMITTED AND PERSECUTED CHRISTIANS

TOUGH-MINDED CHRISTIANS

The world needs tough-minded Christians: Christians who are determined to do God's will, who believe in Jesus Christ as the Son of God, who have a sternness about their beliefs, who are not afraid of criticism, who are not afraid to carry a Bible, and who speak clearly and boldly under the influence of the Holy Spirit. They love their enemies and desire to sacrifice themselves for God, family, and country. We need tough-minded Christians in business, government, schools, and community. We need people who know without a doubt what programs are wrong. We need Christian men in marriage: serving their families, setting limits, and providing godly instructions.

This is the example of Daniel in the den of lions. Daniel refused the decree of King Darius, which was manipulated and set in place by the enemies of Daniel.

Daniel was a shining star in Babylon, accomplishing tasks of government with success but continuing to pray to God as an upright Jew. This caused envy among his peers. As a scheme to put Daniel in his place, they passed a law that could not be altered. The law required everyone to worship the king. If not, the punishment was to throw the offender in the lion's den. Nevertheless, Daniel continued worshipping the one true God, praying three times a day. His adversaries reported this fact to the king. The king was displeased with himself for allowing the passage of such a law.

However, unable to free Daniel, the king gave the command for Daniel to be cast into the den of lions. But the king said to Daniel that his God would deliver him.

The next day, the king rose very early and went in haste to the den of lions, calling to Daniel to discover if God had delivered him. God had. Daniel told the king that God had sent His angel and shut the lions' mouths, because Daniel was found innocent before Him and had done no wrong to the king (see Dn 6:12–22).

Today we seldom experience physical torture and stress— although being held in jail without due process or having an agency of the federal government make inappropriate demands on the citizens is disturbing. Our torture is financial torture. Agencies refuse to complete loan requests, refuse to allow business permits, and require various business reports and records. Our fights are in the courts, conducted with legal briefs. We are thankful to several legal organizations that help us to stand up against the government.

Tough-minded Christians are grounded in faith, the rock of Jesus Christ. They know the Christian doctrines of sin, repentance, forgiveness, sacrifice, sanctification, obedience, thanksgiving, heaven, and glorification. Tough-minded Christians know the testimonies and faithful witness of Abel, who offered to God a more excellent sacrifice than did Cain. By faith Enoch was taken away so that he did not see death. By faith Noah, moved with godly fear, prepared an ark. By faith Abraham obeyed when he was called to go out, not knowing where he was going. By faith Sarah received strength to conceive when she was past age.

Nearly a million Christians have been martyred in the last ten years, a Christian research firm affiliated with Gordon-Conwell Theological Seminary in Massachusetts estimates. Gordon-Conwell's Center for the Study of Global Christianity recently released its annual report on the persecution of Christians, which found that as many as ninety thousand Christians died for their faith in the last year.[1]

Even with these alarming statistics and a fearful future, nevertheless, Christians find joy in their work and in their suffering, knowing that God will never forsake us. There is much work to be done to bring the life of the Lord into the hearts of men with financial miracles.

CHAPTER NINETEEN

CONCLUSION

CONCLUSION

In conclusion, a true financial miracle happens when we become born-again, receiving the "New Financial Nature" with a trust that God provides. We become directed anew to serve others. We become tough-minded, knowing God is in charge. We become prayerful in all circumstances. We become eager to learn God's will for our lives. We become ready for God's call for service. We become an answer to someone's prayer for a financial miracle. We become content with our situation, trusting and hoping in Jesus and our future in heaven.

Our changed nature results in being born again, becoming new creatures in Christ. We are changed like trusting children in order to enter the kingdom. We are renewed by the Holy Spirit and undergo a spiritual recreation in order to have a relationship with God and enter His kingdom.

There is good news for the poor in Christianity, because God loves us regardless of wealth and possessions. People who try to prove that God has blessed them by displaying their possessions have got it wrong. In fact, scripture discusses the deceitfulness of wealth as an alluring temptation. Position, possessions, bank balances, and power are idols. As wealth increases, dependence on God decreases.

When unemployed, keep self-confidence high by doing maintenance projects around the house and by volunteering. In addition attempt to keep government out of your lives. Slothfulness and dependency on government are sins. Keep in mind that government is not responsible for providing for the poor, according to the Bible. Rather, the individual is first responsible for himself and his family; second for his extended family, including in-laws; and third for the church.

Prayers for financial miracles may not be answered because of sin and sinful habits. Remember that George Müller's list of prayer elements includes removal of all aspects of sin from your lives. The man born blind said that God does not hear sinners, but if anyone is a worshipper of God and does His will, God hears him.

Get close to God through religious activities, prayers, and by regular giving. Keep in mind the scripture passage that your heart is where your treasure is. Change that treasure to be first the church.

Divine providence is God's responsibility to sustain creation, making the sun come up each day and the earth keep spinning. We are part of His creation. He promises to help us in our need. He knows you and loves you individually and personally, including the number of hairs on your head. We need to firmly believe, trust, and obey His Word. We need to delight in the Lord's teaching, learning to recognize the financial miracles in our lives. The joy for God is to receive you in heaven, which is your ultimate goal and surpasses all financial suffering.

Imagine the change in our families as the "New Financial Nature" becomes part of the way of life? Discussions and disagreements about money diminish, financial mistakes are forgiven, financial priorities change, individual family members cooperate to find solutions, family members sacrifice for each other, and God as an outside power displays his care and provision. These changes would be a financial miracle.

Imagine the changes as the "New Financial Nature" moves

into in the workplace. Employees would be thankful for their jobs with an understanding that personal services can rise to the level of one's calling from God. Workers would do their very best each day with cooperation and helpfulness. Employers would be thankful for workers and treat them as family. The employer and company owners would expect reasonable compensation for their efforts and investment without greed and power. These changes would be a financial miracle.

Oh, how I imagine the "New Financial Nature" changing communities and governments. Let us pray as in the Lord's Prayer: "thy kingdom come".

END NOTES

Chapter 1—God is powerful and provides

1   John MacArthur, *The MacArthur Bible Commentary* (Nashville: Thomas Nelson, 2005), 1134.

2   Marvin Small, *How to attain Financial Security and Self-Confidence,* (New York: Simon and Schuster, 1953).

3   R. A. Finlayson, *The Illustrated Bible Dictionary,* revision ed. Norman Hillyer (Wheaton: Inter-Varsity Press, Tyndale House Pub, 1980, reprinted 1986). 569.

4   Herbert Lockyer Sr., ed., *Nelson's Illustrated Bible Dictionary,* Guideposts ed. (Nashville: Thomas Nelson, 1986), 425–427.

Chapter 2—God requires participation

1   James D. Spiceland, *Evangelical Dictionary of Theology,* 2nd ed. (Grand Rapids: Baker Academic, 2001), 779.

2   Augustine, *City of God,* as quoted in Spiceland, *Evangelical,* 779.

3   George Müller, *Answers to Prayer,* ed. Lore F. Wilbert (Nashville: B&H Publishing, 2017), 60–64.

Chapter 3—Poverty, good news, and work

1   *Encyclopedia Britannica,* "Poverty," accessed April 21, 2020, https://www.britannica.com/topic/poverty.

2   John Harrington, "From the Solomon Islands to Liberia: These Are the 25 Poorest Countries of the World," *USA Today,* accessed April 21, 2020, https://www.usatoday.com/story/money/2018/11/29/poorest-countries-world-2018/38429473.

3   J. W. McGarvey, *Four-Fold Gospel* (Cincinnati: Standard Publishing Company, 1914), 290.

4   Ralph Drollinger, *Oaks in Office*, vol. 3 (Ventura, CA: Nordskog, 2018), 352–354.

5   Adrian Rodgers, *Practical Christianity,* "A Christian View of Daily Work," LaVonne Neff, Ron Beers, et al eds., (Carol Stream, IL: Tyndale House Pub, 1986), 569.

6   V. Gilbert Beers, *Practical Christianity,* "Service and Spiritual Growth," LaVonne Neff, Ron Beers, et al eds., (Carol Stream, IL: Tyndale House Pub, 1986), 609.

Chapter 4—Financial suffering, persecution, and joy

1   Tremper Longman III and Raymond B. Dillard, *An Introduction to the Old Testament*, 2nd ed. (Grand Rapids, MI: Zondervan, 2006), 139.

2   Longman and Dillard, *Introduction*, 142.

3   *Life Application Bible, New International Version* (Wheaton, IL: Tyndale House Pub. and Grand Rapids: Zondervan Publishing Hs., 1991), 373.

4   Ibid., *Life Application Bible*, 373

5   Richard Wurmbrand, *Tortured for Christ* (Bartlesville, OK: Voice of the Martyrs, 1967), 30.

6   Wurmbrand, *Tortured*, 59.

7   Wurmbrand, *Tortured*, 38.

8   Wurmbrand, *Tortured*, 42.

9   Wurmbrand, *Tortured*, 146.

10   John S. Feinberg, *Evangelical Dictionary of Theology*, 2nd ed. (Grand Rapids, MI: Baker Academic, 2001), 882–3.

11   Joni and Friends, "Mission Statement", accessed May 2, 2023 ttps://www.joniandfriends.org/about/what-we-do/

12   Feinberg, *Evangelical*, 883.

13   Feinberg, *Evangelical*, 883.

Chapter 5—The undeserved favor of God and freedom

1   Chad Brand et al, eds., *Holman Illustrated Bible Dictionary,* "grace", (Nashville: Holman Bible Publishers, 2003).

2   Theodore G. Tappert, translator and editor, *The Book of Concord: The Confessions of the Evangelical Lutheran Church,* "The Augsburg Confession," 1530, (Philadelphia: Fortress Press, 1959), 78-79.

3   The Four Absolutes – The Oxford Group, "What are the absolutes", accessed May 2, 2023, www.jcrecoverycenter.com/blog/the-four-absolutes/

4   Hazelden Betty Ford Foundation, "Twelve Steps of Alcoholics Anonymous," accessed December 22, 2020, https://www. hazeldenbettyford.org/articles/twelve-steps-of-alcoholics-anonymous.
5   Ibid., Hazelden

Chapter 6—Miracles are not free

1   Henrietta C. Mears, *What the Bible Is All About,* "Baal", (Alexander, AZ: Gospel Light Publications, 1983).
2   John Walvood and Roy Zuck, eds., *The Bible Knowledge Commentary, Old Testament* (Colorado Springs, CO, Cook Communications Ministries, 2000). 524.
3   Matthew Henry, *Matthew Henry's Commentary on the Whole Bible,* vol. 2 (Old Tappan, NJ: Fleming H. Revell, originally written 1706), 667.
4   Martin Luther, *Luther's Large Catechism: A Contemporary Translation with Study Questions,* F. Samuel Janzow, trans., (St. Louis, MO: Concordia Publishing, 1978), 13.

Chapter 7—Experiencing miracles from God

1   John Walvood and Roy Zuck, eds., *The Bible Knowledge Commentary, Old Testament* (Colorado Springs, Cook Communications Ministries, 2000). 1585.

Chapter 8—Financial hope and a new heart

1   Matthew Henry, *Matthew Henry's Commentary on the Whole Bible,* vol. 1 (Old Tappan, NJ: Fleming H. Revell, originally written in 1706), 362-3.

Chapter 9—Guilt, forgiveness, and restoration

1   Theodore G. Tappert, translator and editor, *The Book of Concord: The Confessions of the Evangelical Lutheran Church,* "The Small Catechism", 1529, (Philadelphia: Fortress Press, 1959), 342-344.
2   Paul Davis, "Propositions 6", Institute for American Values, January 2012, a pamphlet.
3   *Life Application Bible, New International Version* (Wheaton, IL: Tyndale House Pub. and Grand Rapids: Zondervan Publishing Hs., 1991), 457.
4   *Life Application Bible,* 467.

Chapter 10—Nearer to God through prayer

1   Theodore G. Tappert, translator and editor, *The Book of Concord: The Confessions of the Evangelical Lutheran Church*, "The Large Catechism", 1529, (Philadelphia: Fortress Press, 1959), 415.

2   Matthew George Easton, *Easton's Illustrated Bible Dictionary*, 3rd ed., (London: T. Nelson and Sons, 1897), 574.

3   R. A. Torrey, *How to Obtain Fullness of Power* (Pittsburgh: Whitaker House 1982, 1984). 59–63.

4   George Müller, "Five Conditions of Prevailing Prayer," accessed March 10, 2022, https://www.georgemuller.org/devotional/five-conditions-of-prevailing-prayer1.

5   Graham, Billy, *Answers*, accessed June 1, 2004, https://billygraham.org/grow-your-faith/topics/christian-living/prayer/.

6   Got Questions, "Is the ACTS Formula for Prayer a Good Way to Pray?" accessed April 16, 2018, https://www.gotquestions.org/ACTS-prayer.html.

Chapter 11—Nearer to God through giving

1   *Life Application Bible, New International Version* (Wheaton, IL: Tyndale House Pub. and Grand Rapids: Zondervan Publishing Hs., 1991), 1134.

2   John Walvoord and Roy B. Zuck, eds., *The Bible Knowledge Commentary*: *Old Testament* (Colorado Springs, CO: Cook Communications Ministries, 2000), 976–7.

Chapter 12—Financial worry, planning, and trust

1   John Walvoord and Roy B. Zuck, eds., *The Bible Knowledge Commentary*: *New Testament* (Colorado Springs, CO: David C. Cook, 1983), 33.

2   Albert Barnes and Robert Frew, *Barnes' Notes on the New Testament* 1847, (Grand Rapids: Kregel Publications 1962), comments on Mt 6:32-34.

3   William Barclay, *The Gospel of Matthew*, vol. 1, rev. ed. (Philadelphia: Westminster Press, 1975), 258.

Chapter 13—Socialism, control, and the two kingdoms

1   Terence Ball and Richard Dagger, "Socialism," *Encyclopedia Britannica*, accessed March 1, 2021, https://www.britannica.com/topic/socialism.

2   Ibid. Terence Ball, "Socialism,"

3   Robert Schumacher, *Christian Post*, Wednesday, April 22, 2020, https://www.christianpost.com/voices/why-communist-and-leftist-governments-hate-christianity.html.

4   Jeffery Jones, "U.S. Church Membership Falls Below Majority for First Time", Gallup, Inc., accessed March 29, 2021, https://news.gallup.com/poll/341963/church-membership-falls-below-majority-first-time.aspx.

Chapter 14—Living in the kingdom of God

1   The People of the Book, "How to Enter the Kingdom of God," accessed November 25, 2021, https://www.thepeopleofthebook.org/about/strategy/how-to-enter-the-kingdom-of-god/.

Chapter 15—Financial cares and the spiritually poor

1   Albert Barnes and Robert Frew, *Barnes' Notes on the New Testament* 1847, (Grand Rapids: Kregel Publications 1962), comments on Mt 13:24.

2   Matthew Henry, *Matthew Henry's Commentary on the Whole Bible*, vol. 5 (Old Tappan, NJ: Fleming H. Revell, originally written in 1706), 185–6.

3   Augustine, *Confessions,* as quoted in Crossroads Initiative, accessed December 4, 2021, www.crossroadsinitiative.com/media/articles/ourheartisrestlessuntilitrestsinyou.

4   Martin Luther, *The Place of Trust: Martin Luther on the Sermon on the Mount*, ed. Martin E. Marty (San Francisco: Harper & Row, 1983), 47.

Chapter 16—God knows our thoughts and situation

1   Martin Luther, *Sermons of Martin Luther*, ed. John Nicholas Lenker, vol. 4 (Grand Rapids, MI: Baker Book House, 1988), 223.

Chapter 17—Divine providence and the affairs of nations

1   Herbert Lockyer, ed., *Nelson's Illustrated Bible Dictionary* (Nashville, TN: Thomas Nelson, 1986), 883.

2   Matthew Henry, *Matthew Henry Unabridged*, Luke, Chapter 22 (Grand Rapids: Topics Bible Publisher, 1976), 808.

3   Shekhinah Clinic for the Poor and Destitute, accessed March 4, 2022, https://shekhinahclinic.org.

Chapter 18—Committed and persecuted Christians

1   *The Christian Post,* accessed January 5, 2022, www.christianpost.
    com/news/over-900000-christians-martyred-for-their-faith-in-last-
    10-years-report.html.

Printed in the United States
by Baker & Taylor Publisher Services